T0146736

Inspired by God

An Approach to Biblical Leadership

Ryan Cappadony

WESTBOW
PRESS®
A DIVISION OF THOMAS NELSON
& ZONDERVAN

Unless otherwise stated scriptures are taken from the Holy Bible, New
International Version. NIV. Copyright 1973, 1978, 1984 by International
Bible Society. Used by permission of Zondervan. All rights reserved.
Scripture quotations marked NKJV are taken from the
New King James Version. Copyright 1982 by Thomas
Nelson, Inc. Used by permission. All rights reserved.

WestBow Press books may be ordered through
booksellers or by contacting:

WestBow Press
A Division of Thomas Nelson & Zondervan
1663 Liberty Drive
Bloomington, IN 47403
www.westbowpress.com
1 (866) 928-1240

ISBN: 978-1-5127-9429-8 (sc)
ISBN: 978-1-5127-9428-1 (e)

Library of Congress Control Number: 2017910942

Print information available on the last page.

WestBow Press rev. date: 07/17/2017

For my *Inspirer*.
To my *family*.

Contents

Preface

Why Another Book on Leadership?

As a retiree of the US Armed Forces, a single-staff pastor, an associate pastor, and an administrative pastor, I have had my ups and downs when it comes to leadership. During my tenure in the military, I was privileged to work beside, learn from, and teach many different people from many different backgrounds under many different circumstances. In some instances it was peaceful, everyday work activities. In other instances it was training scenarios in a garrison environment. Still other instances were in the harsh realities of combat operations in foreign countries. One thing I noticed was the constant barrage of leadership successes and failures.

The military does a wonderful job of teaching practical leadership to young recruits and senior officers alike. The armed forces does this because its military leaders recognize the need for continuous professional development. That is to say that not only technical skills are enhanced with increasing rank and responsibility, but leadership skills are as well. The inundation of leadership is rampant in both young noncommissioned officers and young officers. The military begins by indoctrinating young men and women into roles and scenarios that test their mettle and force them to think beyond anything they have ever done. A live scenario might include a belligerent young service member who is fed up with authority and is not afraid to let everyone know their blatant disregard and disrespect for it. The scenario is introduced to a member and the member must figure out what they are to do to motivate this "problem follower." If the member is successful, then great; but if they are not successful, what follows is a long discussion of what they could have done differently.

To be sure, the military has had tremendous success with building some fine leaders. The problem is that everything is so fast-paced that service members only know that they should do things differently if they get it wrong and don't really know what they did if they get it right. They are basing their leadership off a long practical examination of trial and error. Every once in a while, there are leadership classes that come in the form of ethics, values, and very abbreviated styles-type classes, which are more often outdated than not. The reality is that every service member is a leader. But the other reality is that they don't really know why much of the time.

At the end of my military career, I found something different—especially when I stepped into the leadership role of a church. I was challenged in a different way. Sure, I was able to hold meetings and keep them on track. I was able to direct events and delegate appropriately. I was basing my leadership off a military career that worked well for me in that environment. Soon I found that this was not always the best way to handle a congregation of longtime Christians. It was fine for some scenarios but not for all.

I began to search books for spiritual leadership, godly leadership, Christ-centered leadership, biblical leadership. I certainly found them, and they were (and continue to be) very helpful. They demonstrated great ways to turn to Scripture and find out how the giants of faith handled situations. Something was still missing, however.

The thing about seminary is that it is truly great for learning and understanding the Bible. I will always contend that there is no greater task, or joy, than sharing the gospel of Jesus Christ. That being said, it is essential to know, as accurately as possible, what the gospel entails and how to shepherd God's people. But how does one lead them? This truly became the task for me. Here I was, a decent military leader and a decent church leader, but I still did not understand what I was doing, so I began a journey of working toward examining organizational leadership. What I found was eye-opening and foundational to how I perceive leadership today.

It's amazing how many church leaders there are struggling with leading a congregation, especially single-staff pastors. That's not to say that there aren't multi-staff churches struggling as well, because there are many. Oftentimes we see these church leaders seeking advice and leadership from the savvy secular world because they see the successes of their companies. Let's just think about that for a second and be completely candid about it. If a pastor sees himself as a CEO, then he should revisit the Bible. Jesus did not tell Peter to be the chief executive officer of his sheep. Churches are not businesses to be run for trade or merchandise. The Bible is very clear:

> Do not conform any longer to the pattern
> of this world, but be transformed by the
> renewing of your mind. Then you will be
> able to test and approve what God's will
> is—His good, pleasing and perfect will.
> (Romans 12:2)

If we are busy thinking ourselves CEOs of "church business," then have we really transformed ourselves from the thinking of this world? To be sure, church is not a secular business; it is an organization of people doing God's work for God's kingdom. And just as Scripture teaches, if we are not seeking godly wisdom, then we will not know God's wisdom. This brings me back to where I left off, studying organizational leadership.

Leadership is full of studies, theories, practices, and skills that transcend the secular. Why? Because the aforementioned may be found in God's word. This book is a step beyond any other biblical leadership book you might read. It is where the Bible meets academics and goes straight back to the Bible. It is designed to give Christian leaders, of all sorts, the ability to know what they are doing and why they are doing it and examine how their leadership can be used to help further God's kingdom. It will explain how leadership is biblical and help you to recognize your own leadership style and practices as well as identify others' so you can help them in developing their leadership styles. After all, isn't this a part of shepherding? Isn't this a part of discipling? We should be in constant examination of ourselves, and we need to know enough of what we are seeing to be able to effectively and biblically guide others through this process of sanctification.

One of my favorite Psalms is the first one.

> Blessed is the man who does not walk in the counsel of the wicked or stand in the way of sinners or sit in the seat of mockers. But his delight is in the law of the Lord, and on His law he meditates day and night. (Psalm 1:1–2)

What is the opposite of God and His laws? If we aren't taking a close examination of ourselves and where our information is coming from, then are we truly delighting in His laws, His ways? Contrary to some Christian beliefs, talk shows and news programs should not be the greatest sources for biblical wisdom. Leadership is no different in this respect. It is critical we search the Bible for our leadership, especially since it affects so much of whom we are and what we should be doing for God's kingdom.

Ryan J. Cappadony
North Bend, Oregon, USA
December 2016

Acknowledgments

Many people are responsible for the writing of *Inspired by God*. Although I am sure to miss many, there are a number of people I would like to thank for their direct and indirect contributions to this work. First, I wish to thank all the men and women of the US Armed Forces who selflessly give of their time to ensure that others may have some. The sacrifices made are of value, and I hope each service member realizes his or her importance and potential.

All of the brave souls I had the pleasure of serving with are always on my mind and in my heart. For the men and women I was privileged to lead, thank you. If I could do more for you, it would still not be enough. Your attention laid the groundwork for my leadership studies and had an immense impact on this book.

I also want to thank the congregations that have taught me many lessons in leadership. It is through the leading of godly people that I first felt the desire to even pen such a work.

I wish to thank the faculty and staff of Regent University for their support through my graduate years. A particular acknowledgment goes to the faculty and staff of Regent University's School of Business and Leadership. But most of all, I want to thank Dr. Jeff Suderman for his guidance, encouragement, and instruction, without whom I would not have finished such a work as this.

For my family, I can only say that I love each one of you in a way that surpasses my understanding. Your continuous support throughout my life always inspires me, and I cannot thank you enough—especially my wife, Amy, and three children.

More than any, I want to thank my God. God brought me the love of the Father through the redemption of Jesus Christ, who works in me by the Holy Spirit. God, You are my Inspirer, and it is because of You that this book is written.

1

From the Start

What Is Leadership?

J. Oswald Sanders wrote that leadership is one's ability to influence others—and that great leaders know this.[1] This sentiment seems in agreement with those who practice leadership and those who try to understand leadership. But have we also considered that leadership is foundational to thriving organizations? Most believe that leadership is the single most important factor in the success or failure of institutions.[2]

I already stated that the church is not a business, but it is an organization. It is an institution. It is an organization because Christians are formed together for a particular purpose. It is an institution because it is an organization devoted to a particular cause and established by Jesus Christ. Clearly Jesus is viewed as the head, and that determines Him as the overall leader of the Christian organization.[3] But recall that Jesus appointed others to carry on His leadership.

To help illustrate this, take a look at John 21:20–23. Peter seems to be worried about what is going to happen with John. He looks at Jesus and says, "What about him?" Jesus simply says, "Don't worry about him. I have him doing other things. You just follow My leadership." Of course, this is a paraphrase, but now fast-forward to the book of Acts. Peter has seen standing in front of a large crowd, and he is giving an amazing and inspirational speech about salvation.[4] The leader, Jesus, turned over the reins after building and inspiring another leader, Peter. We need to understand that the Holy Spirit is very involved here. But there is also something very fundamental about leadership that just transpired from John's gospel to Luke's account in Acts. There should be no wonder why leadership experts Bass and Stodgill would begin their classic *Handbook on Leadership* with an understanding that leaders existed in the Old and New Testaments.[5] God knows how to lead, and He has been producing great leaders for longer than we have been reading books on leadership.

But we are still left with the question, what is leadership? Is it simple inspiration, or is it delegation? Is it a mentor—protégé project? Peter Northouse quotes Stodgill by stating that there are numerous definitions of leadership—almost as many definitions as those who try to define it.[6] It seems that leadership means many different things to many different people. It almost seems ambiguous.

For many, defining leadership is a lot like trying to clarify and define love. That is, we know it when we feel it or when we see it, but finding the right words to describe or define it is entirely different.[7] But there is good news. There is a way to define and describe love:

> Dear friends, let us love one another, for love comes from God. Everyone who loves has been born of God and knows God. Whoever does not love does not know God, because God is love. This is how God showed His love among us: He sent His one and only Son into the world that we might live through Him. This is love: not that we loved God, but that He loved us and sent His Son as an atoning sacrifice for our sins. Dear friends, since God so loved us, we also ought to love one another. No one has ever seen God; but if we love one another, God lives in us and His love is made complete in us. (1 John 4:7–12)

It stands to reason that if we can describe and define something as ubiquitous yet elusive to us as love by equating it to God and His characteristics, then we should be able to describe and define leadership by the same token. That is to say that if we pore over the Bible, we have the very description and definition of leadership found of and in God. And just as those who have God in them are recognizable by the measure of love they demonstrate toward God and one another, those who demonstrate biblical leadership are recognizable to have God in them as well.

For example, when Jesus is teaching His disciples how to pray in Matthew 6, He regards the Father as a leader. Notice what Jesus is suggesting—that God leads us away from the temptation brought about by the weakness of flesh and influenced by the evil one. Humankind is susceptible to temptation (James 1:14). But since the Bible tells us that God cannot be tempted by evil, nor does He tempt anyone (see James 1:13), we must declare that God has nothing to do with temptation itself other than to bring us out of or away from it.[8] Consider that for a moment. James 1:13–15 tells us that temptation, in and of itself, is not a sin, but it gives birth to sin. Recall that Jesus was tempted in the wilderness but did not sin.[9] You and I are not built that way thanks to Adam, but we do have someone to lead us in the right direction—God is that leader. Likewise, we have Christian brothers and sisters around us who exude godly character and help us do the same. This is how we are able to see the godly attribute of leadership. The reason we seek Christian leadership is because Christians around us—and before us—follow God's mentorship. This, then, provides the generic definition of biblical leadership: God's ability to influence His people toward a shared cause of righteousness for His kingdom.

Implicit v. Explicit

Implied leadership is a theoretical view of personal cognitive comparisons between what the observer sees and expects out of different people based on certain criteria such as gender, nationality, position, age, etc.

Followers have an expectation that leaders will exude certain characteristics based on particular behaviors; this expectation leads to perceived leadership that encompasses the leader's expressed style as observed by followers. The result is either a confirmation of acceptance or a rejection to follow based on what followers see and perceive from the leader.[10] What all this means is that followers see certain leadership characteristics that they like, and they see characteristics that they dislike. People choose to pick out admirable qualities in an attempt to adopt them as their own. Leadership qualities perceived as negative are avoided as useful personal tools.

Each of us can most likely recall a person who positively influenced us. Perhaps right now you are thinking about a person who holds or held those admirable qualities—qualities you either aspire to adopt or have adopted. What often stems from this is a leadership style that becomes personal to an individual, but the individual could probably not tell anyone what style it falls under beyond being his or her own. I don't want this to sound as though it is bad, however. My guess is that Moses did not have leadership books to study so he could understand how to improve his style. In fact, if Moses were to be interviewed for this book, he might attribute all his learned leadership to God. And we should expect nothing less from the most humble man. Besides, it would not be an incorrect answer, yet we can still see the people God put in Moses's life to help him develop a leadership style and even further develop the people he led.

First, we should be able to see that implicit leadership is a God-given characteristic that people help bring out.

Recall the encounter of Moses with the burning bush. Exodus 3:10–12 gives us a glimpse of what I mean. God tells Moses that He is sending him to Pharaoh to lead the Israelites out of Egypt. Moses quickly rebuts with an incredulous attitude. But God assures Moses that He will be with him. This is often how implicit leadership begins. A leader sees a potential follower, and the follower, although having much admiration for the leader, has doubts about whether he or she can perform to those standards. Yet the follower cannot help but be drawn to these inexplicable qualities, and he or she will have a desire to want to do right by the leader. This was the beginning of Moses's leadership transformation— albeit some of his Egyptian background would come to his aid. But we must take notice of the people who surrounded Moses as he developed his leadership style.

Aaron was sent to speak for Moses as his prophet.[11] Jethro, Moses's father-in-law, gave advice and blessings to Moses on multiple occasions.[12] And of course, there were the Israelites. All of these had a great influence on Moses as he led. Although they should have been more attentive of their own obedience to God, the people turned to Moses for answers. When they felt trapped after fleeing Pharaoh, it was Moses they turned to and blamed even though they first cried out to God.[13] When the Israelites were thirsty, they complained to their leader, Moses.[14] When the Israelites were hungry, who did they blame? Yes, Moses.[15] But we notice that Moses continued on. Moses gained his strength and knowledge from the Lord. The people around him honed those skills that became ever important in leading the Israelites out of captivity and straight to the place God wanted them. We should seek to wonder how we respond to complaints and if we are leading people where God wants them to be, despite the complaints.

The first thing we need to do is figure out what God-given attributes we are given and develop those. Then we need to figure out what God's direct purpose for us is and seek God to institute this. Next we need to surround ourselves with people who will define those attributes and purpose. Remember that Moses said he was not eloquent in speech. God appointed Aaron to do this for him, at least for a little while. After some time, Moses became very capable to speak on his own.[16] There were no textbooks to help with Moses's leadership style—only the mentorship of God. Moses would go on to mentor a very capable protégé to lead the next generation of Israelites into the Promised Land. That's what implicit leadership is—taking the good characteristics of what you know and see and are taught and making them yours to lead others through a rising of followership.

The contrast, or at least a different approach, is explicit leadership. By definition the term *explicit* means to reveal without question or ambiguity. There is no doubt to what is expected or understood by the individual, and there is no doubt who has been put in charge. This is the real essence of explicit leadership. Some prefer to call it appointed leadership just as they prefer to call implicit leadership emergent leadership. I tend to look more at the terms *implicit* and *explicit* because they not only define the appointment of position, but they also define the characteristics of the individual. It should also be noted that there are good sides and bad sides to both types, but explicit leadership receives far more scrutiny from followers. One of the greatest illustrations of this is the military or para-military environments.

The military promotes people based on a number of factors, and each branch does it a little differently. But it is expected that with each successive rank achieved, there is a new leadership position filled. Sometimes those promoted are not the best suited for leadership positions. This type of explicit leadership can be dangerous if the newly appointed leader has no real desire to lead, only a desire to be in charge. This is known as position power.[17] Position power gives the explicit leader the ability to reward, punish, change, or gain compliance from followers.[18] It can be very dangerous in the wrong hands or with dubious motives. Be sure, as well, that plans do not have to begin with dubiousness; they can evolve into them. The wrong seed sown into the heart of a leader can wreak havoc on the followers.

King Saul is an example of this. Recall that he was appointed because the Israelites wanted a king to rule over them, like the other nations.[19] Samuel knew better. He knew that their real Leader was God. Nevertheless, as an explicit leader, Saul fell into power position. Eventually, Saul was rejected by God as king for his arrogance and rebellion.[20] It seems his leadership went to his head.

There is a good outcome of this type of leadership. Those who refuse to give in to vainglories are far more deserving of followers. It is important to see leadership as a privilege and not a hindrance of position or a chance to enact revenge.

The book of Genesis tells a remarkable tale of forgiveness and reconciliation. Joseph was given a rough season, to say the least. But after some maturity and finding some humility, God knew it was time to move Joseph into a different phase. Joseph was appointed the chief of Egypt. He did not rise through the ranks as someone to follow; he was a prisoner, after all. He was shown favor by Pharaoh for interpreting a dream.[21] As a result, Joseph was strictly promoted to his position of authority. We should suppose there were at least some who did not like this and felt it was unfair. Joseph was happy to accept and went straight to work. Things were going very well for Joseph—a loving wife, great kids, a happy Pharaoh, plenty of food for future famines, and satisfied constituents. Joseph was doing all right. That is, of course, until the brothers that brought him such pain and suffering for so long, the brothers who tore Joseph away from his loving mother and father, came looking for food. Joseph had not been prepared for this.

Leadership often takes us on a path of uncertainty. Rest assured, whenever there are people involved, especially many people, there will be heartache, there will be pain; but there can also be joy and triumph. As leaders, the latter is what we strive for, but the former is what helps to mold us.

Joseph could have used his power position to rid himself of all his brothers. They deserved it, didn't they? They put him through pain and suffering. They treated him like a second-rate citizen, to say nothing of the sibling abandonment. Joseph would have been well within his rights to act as harshly toward them as they did him, wouldn't he? Not according to God. Joseph decided to act as his leader, merciful and compassionate. Joseph's actions moved beyond being vengeful and into real leadership. In the end, he sought the joy and triumph that can accompany leadership.

> His brothers came and threw themselves down before him. "We are your slaves," they said. But Joseph said to them, "Don't be afraid. Am I in the place of God? You intended to harm me, but God intended it for good to accomplish what is now being done, the saving of many lives. So then, don't be afraid. I will provide for you and your children." And he reassured them and spoke kindly to them. (Genesis 50:18–21)

It should not take much to see the difference of attitude between Joseph and Saul. Both were recipients of explicit leadership, yet one allowed position power to overthrow the best of judgments for personal gain. Satan, after all, is very good at extorting and distorting position power.

The Relevance of Biblical Leadership

To this point we have given a short introduction of biblical leadership. Hopefully much has been demonstrated about the Bible, leadership, and how one can gain practical knowledge of such an academic subject. Yet we have not truly entered into the academics of it. There is much more to discover, and I suppose there will be much to leave out. The purpose of this book is not to bog the reader down with academia but to help the reader see the value of the Bible within academia. Too often we treat the Bible as an academic textbook, but it is not. Contained within the Bible is a mountain of godly wisdom and knowledge for the everyday person of faith. We do not read the Bible for strict wisdom and knowledge, however. We read it to discover more of God. We read it to discover the scarlet thread that runs through it and is revealed through our Savior, Jesus Christ.

This book, then, is a nod to the leadership potential in all Christ-followers. It is not meant as a replacement for searching the Scriptures. It is meant to demonstrate the versatility of the Bible and illustrate the importance of biblical leadership. It is also meant as an aid in reference to scholars, pastors, lay leaders, students, and anyone interested in enriching their biblical leadership to help them be better Christian leaders in the world for God's kingdom.

Many attempt to put a face on leadership. We observe them through time and strive to emulate them. We should never overlook the fact that the very face of leadership died on a cross long ago, but then rose again so we could see what unconditional leadership is all about. The very face of leadership sits on a throne at the present. And as far as I can discern, it has no end.

Chapter Notes

1   J. O. Sanders, *Spiritual Leadership: Principles of Excellence for Every Believer* (Chicago: Moody Publishers, 2007), 27.

2   B. Bass and R. Stogdill, *Bass & Stogdill's Handbook of Leadership: Theory, Research, and Managerial Applications* (New York: The Free Press, 1990), 8.

3   Cf. Colossians 1:18

4   Cf. Acts 2:14–42

5   Bass and Stogdill, *Bass & Stogdill's Handbook of Leadership*, 7.

6   P. Northouse, *Leadership: Theory and Practice*, seventh ed. (Los Angeles, CA: Sage, 2015), 2.

7   W. Burke, *Organization Change: Theory and Practice*, fourth ed. (Los Angeles, CA: Sage, 2014), 279–80.

8   For a more complete explanation, see Frank Gaebelein, ed., *The Expositor's Bible Commentary*, vol. 5 (Grand Rapids, MI: Zondervan, 1984), 173–74.

9   Cf. Matthew 4:1–11, Mark 1:12–13, Luke 4:1–13

10 R. M. Stock and G. Ozbek-Pothoff, "Implicit leadership in an intercultural context: theory extension and empirical investigation," *International Journal of Human Resource Management* 25, no. 2 (2014): 1651–68. R. M. Stock and G. Ozbek-Pothoff deliver a case study involving implicit leadership theory (ILT) that helps to confirm the wide use of ILT within an intercultural setting.

11 See Exodus 4:14–16, 7:1

12 See Exodus 3:1, 4:18, and especially 18:1–27

13 Exodus 14:10–12

14 Exodus 15:22–24

15 Exodus 16:2–3

16 See Exodus 16:9, 16:15–17, 20:18–20. Moses had grown so close to God that he now spoke as a prophet. The Israelites feared the Lord, but they also trusted Moses's relationship with the Lord enough to hear what he had to say. This is quite a turn-around from Moses's first encounter with God in the bush.

[17] P. Northouse, *Leadership: Theory and Practice*, seventh edition, (Los Angeles, CA: Sage, 2015), 16.

[18] R. Kreitner and A. Kinicki, *Organizational Behavior*, tenth edition, (New York: McGraw-Hill Irvine), 472.

[19] 1 Samuel 8:4–5

[20] 1 Samuel 15:23

[21] See Genesis 41, especially 41:41

2

Moving through Time

Leadership has a way of defining itself through history. Although there are times we do not see those definitions until they are pointed out to us, we still recognize something extraordinary when it happens. Stories told open our senses to the way certain people handled situations. There is a perception of what was successful and what was not. Each of these stories, in their own way, teaches us something.

In this chapter, we will explore how leadership took effect throughout the church at large by identifying four church ages: early church, Reformation church, Enlightenment church, and modern church. As we retell stories past, there should be more than a sense of wonder; there should be a sense of understanding of how we see leadership then and to how it translates into what we now know. One of the beautiful things about leadership is that no matter how far removed from certain time periods, it really does not change.

Lessons from the Early Church Age

In AD 96 a letter from Clement made its way to the congregation in Corinth. Apparently there was an uproar and subsequent scandal that came from some younger men removing the existing elders in the Corinthian church. Clement sough to restore unity by declaring that the church should be run by a plurality of elders, a plurality of leaders. In doing so, Clement, a presbyter-bishop himself, sought to encourage the Corinthians toward a peaceable solution. He spoke of the gentleness and humility of those who should lead the congregation toward a closer relationship with Christ.[1]

What is really demonstrated here, with regard to leadership, is the way in which the situation was handled. Clement could have been harsher with those who sought to "overthrow" the current leadership. Instead, Clement decided to speak to them in the same manner in which he stated they should act.

In Paul's letter to Philemon, we see a similar attitude demonstrated.

> Therefore, although in Christ I could be bold and order you to do what you ought to do, yet I appeal to you on the basis of love. (Philemon 8–9a)

How easy would it have been for Paul, as an elder and apostle, to just tell Philemon he had to comply? Paul understood that position is not for abuse. In a very real way, Paul was explicitly appointed as an apostle by

Jesus Himself. But to use that as an excuse to motivate someone to do what was right was not the way to lead Philemon. Clement was faced with the same dilemma. He too chose to appeal through humble leadership rather than position power.

Perhaps part of Clement's leadership style stemmed from his knowledge of the times. Clement was well versed in the Greek philosophies and classical literatures. But he was also a very astute Bible scholar.[2] He paid attention to the young students of Rome and Athens, who, as it were, became familiar with a gnostic-type Christianity. Clement's goal was "to win not arguments, but men to Christ, and lead them to salvation."[3] As a leader, Clement was very aware of his surroundings and competing influences. He took the time to know what others needed and the way they thought. This should resonate with our understanding of the way Paul presented the gospel to the Athenians in Acts 17. It should also resonate with our understanding of the way each of us approaches our own situations, especially with regard to the saving message of Jesus Christ.

Clement was not the only early church leader. John of Antioch was also very influential in his leadership style. He was given the nickname of Chrysostom, which means "Of Golden Tongue," so most know him as John Chrysostom.[4] What makes him notable as an early church leader is his eloquent and outspoken speech, his firm love for God, and his fervent desire to make the priesthood godly.

Chrysostom had the ability to rally congregations with his sermons. People would intently listen and often applaud his messages. But let's be clear—Chrysostom was not about fame and notoriety. In fact, he was appalled at the notion of it. Chrysostom received applause because his messages were deeply biblical, pastoral in nature, very direct, and simplistic.[5] To be sure, anyone who is direct is going to be met with defense, but the truth is that many want someone to be direct. Followers don't like ambiguity, and they don't like fake. This is what made Chrysostom a leader.

Chrysostom was so direct that he made known his dislike for the priesthood during the fourth century. He saw it being abused in some instances and posited that the priesthood was a direct link to Christ and His people. He found no greater calling than the priesthood, yet he also had disdain for the humans who would make it less than what he thought Jesus instructed Peter to do with it: to be a godly shepherd to the sheep. For Chrysostom, the priesthood was a celestial realm because the priest needed to be of heavenly acumen, not worldly.[6] No matter where one stands theologically, the point is that Chrysostom truly believed what he said, he walked what he spoke, and he made no apologies for asserting Christ as the love of his life. Today we would term this authentic leadership.

James Kouzes and Barry Posner declare that the most admired characteristics in leaders have gone roughly unchanged for a long period of time. At the top of a long list of admired traits is *honest, forward-looking, competent, and inspiring.*[7] Considering what has been presented about Chrysostom, it is safe to assume that he demonstrated these characteristics. He was very honest in word and deed, he considered the future of the church, he was adept in the Bible and pastoral care, and he could inspire a crowd with simple homilies.

Reformation Leadership

Anyone would be remiss to leave Martin Luther out of the Reformation period. His work presented a base upon which others have moved and carried forward. We often view Luther as this great and formidable figure standing atop the Reformation in pure might and glory, but to God's glory, we must first understand Luther's faults that made him inexplicably human and imperfect.

We celebrate the passion of Martin Luther and his willingness to proclaim God's revelations to him. To be sure, Luther's contribution to Protestant genius is impressive when we consider he managed to create a sermon, lecture, treatise, or biblical exposition on the average of once every three weeks.[8] This is least to say that he was also able to translate the New Testament into the German language, while under intense pressures of threat and inner turmoil, in eleven weeks![9] It was Luther's mind and boldness that flocked the masses toward a change in the way God was portrayed to the everyday person. Martin Luther was undoubtedly a leader. He moved people to take a stand for their Christian rights as God's children. He inspired others to step toward other reformations within the confines of their own struggles. Not one Protestant is left doubting that God raised Luther at just the right time to effect a much-needed change in society and church. Beyond his fervency for grace alone, how was his attitude of Christian living?

Martyn Lloyd-Jones said on the 450th anniversary of Martin Luther's Ninety-Five Theses that Luther was prone to suffer bouts of depression and was a hypochondriac, particularly with respect to his bowels.[10] From a leadership perspective, this behavior almost seems personable. After all, what follower does not want a leader they can relate to? But we must also consider Luther's crass speech projected at his congregants under differing views. For example, after some of the Protestant reforms had taken place, some parents concluded that the Catholic Church and its weaknesses spilled into educational institutes, thereby prompting parents to pull their children from school. Martin Luther addressed this issue with the same vigor as he did in his defense for his theses. He said that parents who did not see to their children's education were "no parents at all but despicable hogs and venomous beasts, devouring their own young."[11]

The point of this is not to only demonstrate the imperfections of Martin Luther but to demonstrate the complexities of leadership. Martin Luther was and will remain a formidable figure in both Protestant and Catholic circles. Despite his direct speech and behavior, there is still something to be said for his diligence and theological acumen. There was a love in his heart for God that could not be satisfied by his own cravings although he seemed to relentlessly pursue them. This really lays claim to what church leaders often do to themselves. We take personal responsibility for what should be reserved for God. Luther's internal compass was sometimes the Holy Spirit and other times his personal spirit. Luther's attitude seems to be in contrast to what we think of as far as Christlike behavior. Where were the fruits of the Spirit, after all? Where was the grace that he so fervently believed was the only way anyone could be saved? In the end, Luther, much like many of us in leadership, acted out exactly as Paul wrote,

> So I find this law at work: When I want to do good, evil is right there with me. For in my inner being, I delight in God's law, but I see another law at work in the members of my body, waging war against the law of my mind and making me a prisoner of the law of sin at work within my members. What a wretched man am I! Who will rescue me from this body of death? Thanks be to God—through Jesus Christ our Lord! (Romans 7:21–25)

Today's biblical leaders find themselves emulating the candor of Luther to a fault. We should not point fingers at him unless we are willing to discover our own shortcomings and areas for improvement. In fact, I recall writing a twenty-page leadership assessment on myself. I must say that I did not fare as loving as I would like to think I am because my own candor often gets in the way, even when I think I am saying what I think needs to be said. I thank God through Jesus Christ all the time for His grace and mercy!

Leadership in the Age of Enlightenment

The Age of Enlightenment or Age of Reason, as fondly referred by its adherents, lasted from about 1685 to 1815. To be sure, it was not an instantaneous period that stemmed from one brilliant idea. On the contrary, it was the product of the inculcation of a society without the guidance of God. Not that God did not exist, necessarily (although for some this may have been true), but more of a thought that God stayed Himself from the affairs of humankind. And since God stayed Himself, humankind was free to move about as he wished and was obliged to do.[12]

To assume that leadership during the Enlightenment era ceased to exist or persist is grossly inaccurate. Leadership was alive and well during this time. In fact, it was this time, as in many others, that innovation became a product of thought, especially if we consider that innovation is really a mechanism of change.[13] In order for any of the leaders, godly or not, they had to effect innovation. In essence, they had to effect change.

Change is often associated with the transformational leader. It is someone who can transform followers by initiating and continuing inspiration through thought and action. We will cover transformational leadership in more detail in chapter four. But suffice it to say that both Christian and non-Christian, godly and ungodly leaders were transformational, to some degree, in the direction of the world and society during this time.

Voltaire, for example, inspires philosophers and ethical sojourners to this day; albeit, Voltaire was not exactly fond of Judaism or Christianity. Voltaire's works made way for what we call cultural anthropology today but had little interest in defining Christianity as anything other than a sect of Judaism and loathsomely ridiculous superstition.[14] As far as historians are concerned, Voltaire shaped his time and that which was to come.[15]

Voltaire was not alone in this age that consumed "thought" and "reason." There were others who sought to lead a secularly humanistic society into the furrows of intelligence. Rousseau, Montesquieu, Hume, Locke, and Thomas Paine were some of leaders ushering in the celebration of human intellect over any other. But there were others conforming to a different kind of transformational leadership as well.

Never does the thought of a brooding figure come to mind when thinking of John Wesley. He was, however, formidable in theology and the way in which he presented his theology. He dared to challenge many with his unwavering drive to share a theology that would become known as Methodism because of the methodical ways in which John and Charles Wesley conducted studies and sacraments.[16] It was this kind of godly leadership that spurred generations to examine their theology and connect with God. It was also the kind of godly leadership that was able to stand up against such ungodly acts as human slavery.

John Wesley was on William Wilberforce's side in the quest to end slavery in Britain and if possible, America as well. In fact, Wesley had written a letter to Wilberforce not long before his death encouraging Wilberforce to continue his fight in the pursuit of abolition. It was Wesley's "sophisticated theological reasoning" that some suggest was a great encouragement to Wilberforce.[17] Although this sentiment may have merit, it was more so the transformational-style leadership that Wesley displayed to help drive William Wilberforce to project his own transformational leadership.

Even in the midst of receiving encouragement, however, William Wilberforce and his Clapham Community (a hamlet some three miles from London) were demonstrating what true transformational leadership can accomplish. After centuries of slave trade and just four days before William Wilberforce died, the Emancipation Act of 1833 was passed.[18] As Bruce Shelley writes, "For this reason above all others, the Clapham Sect remains the shining example of how a society—perhaps the world itself—can be influenced by a few men of ability and devotion."[19]

> Trust in the Lord and do good; dwell in the land and enjoy safe pasture. Delight yourself in the Lord and He will give you the desires of your heart. Commit your way to the Lord; trust in Him and He will do this; He will make your righteousness shine like the dawn, the justice of your cause like the noonday sun. (Psalm 37:3–6)

Leading toward God's Kingdom

One of the great difficulties in history is trying to separate transitions and movements. There is a great mixture of complexities that intertwine and weave to make what we perceive today. To say that the Reformation was something that came about in 1521 as the result of a single act of defiance is most certainly not the complete story. There were events and conditions that led to it, just as there was through the Enlightenment. But it was also eras such as the Enlightenment that paved for more reform, such as the Great Awakening and twentieth-century theology. And do we realize that at the center of these movements are leaders that were inspired by God? Faith, as inspiration, is a great motivator. Imagine what might have happened if Noah had not been moved by faith. Or that the very faith that moved Noah to lead at least his family through the largest earthly catastrophe was the same faith that moved a young woman to reach for just a piece of Jesus's clothing. When we are inspired by God, we demonstrate faith.

Today we have organizations that take the idea of biblical leadership and move it into a new direction. For God's sake, we should hope it is for the furtherance of the gospel. You may draw your own conclusions, but they are worth mentioning just the same.

For example, there is the Global Leadership Summit that was instituted by megachurch founder Bill Hybels. The whole premise of this summit is the presentation of leadership topics from church and business leaders to crowds of hundreds of thousands covering practical advice for those wanting to be better leaders. Since there are pastors who are often called to speak, you can rest assured there will be talk about God; but to what extent is up to the hearer.[20] This actually brings us to a point of observation. If any leader is going to succeed for God's kingdom, he or she must be an avid listener.

An avid listener is one who listens to feedback with the understanding that the feedback will be taken willingly and absolutely, no matter how candid the feedback is.[21] This should ring the bells of all church leaders. Part of the reason is because church leaders, and especially pastors, have a habit of telling everyone to listen to God. Well intentioned and true as this is, how often do we actually heed this wisdom?

Take Jonah, for example. We all know the story, and to some credit, Jonah did hear God well enough to carry out what He wanted Jonah to do. But hearing and listening do not equate. The difference between hearing God and listening to God is simply getting the point. Getting the point means we take action on what was articulated. God told Jonah to go into Nineveh and preach repentance. He did just that and still had the audacity to get angry toward God's compassion. After all the wonderful things that Jonah witnessed, including his own comfort in the hot sun, he still didn't get the point.

Listening is one of the greatest tools we have in leadership. If we are not taking the time to listen to God, as our leader, how will we take the time to listen to those we lead, especially when we are confident that God listens to us? Followers want to know you are actively listening to what they have to say.

To be sure, Jonah's work was missionary work. Missionaries have a responsibility, as does anyone seeking to assimilate in other countries, to learn the culture they are entering. Part of this is communication—in particular, listening. If anyone is to build God's kingdom, then they must ask questions, listen to the answers, and then act on them appropriately.[22] This values the relationship more than you'll ever realize. Can we imagine if "new" Protestants did not listen to what the church reformers had to say? Can we imagine what might have happened if people like Jonathan Edwards had not preached according to what God had him preach? The possibilities are endless, but the point remains the same:

> If My people would but listen to Me, if Israel would follow My ways, how quickly would I subdue their enemies and turn My hand against their foes! (Psalm 81:13–14)

Chapter Notes

1   E. Englebrecht, ed, *The Church from Age to Age: A History from Galilee to Global Christianity* (Saint Louis, MO: Concordia Publishing House, 2011), 27.

2   B. Shelley, *Church History in Plain Language*, third edition (Nashville, TN: Thomas Nelson, 2008), 81.

3   Ibid.

4   E. Engelbrecht, ed., *The Church from Age to Age*, 120.

5   Ibid.

6   R. Valantasis, "Body, hierarchy, and leadership in Chrysostom's 'On the Priesthood," *Greek Orthodox Theological Review*, 30(4): pp. 455–71 (1985).

[7] J. Kouzes and B. Posner, *The Leadership Challenge*, fifth edition. (San Francisco, CA: Wiley, 2012), 34–35.

[8] M. Noll, *Turning Points: Decisive Moments in the History of Christianity*, second edition (Grand Rapids, MI: Baker Academic, 2000), 164.

[9] P. Matheson, ed. *Reformation Christianity* in A People's History of Christianity, vol. 5, (Minneapolis, MN: Augsburg Fortress Press, 2010), 1.

[10] M. Noll, *Turning Points: Decisive Moments in the History of Christianity*, second edition, (Grand Rapids, MI: Baker Academic, 2000), 165. Noll quotes Lloyd-Jones, *Luther and His Message for Today* in Evangelical Press, 1968.

[11] M. Noll, *Turning Points*, 164. Message by Martin Luther entitled, "A Sermon on Keeping Children in School."

[12] History Staff, "Enlightenment," retrieved from History.com, 2009. The article gives an overview of the major events and people from the Enlightenment era.

[13] G. Oster, *The Light Prize: Perspectives on Christian Innovation*, (Virginia Beach, VA: Positive Signs Media, 2011).

[14] A. Arkush, "Voltaire on Judaism and Christianity," *ASJ Review, 18*(2): 223–43, (1993).

[15] R. Darnton, "Voltaire, Historian," *Raritan, 35*(2): 20–28, (2015), Rutgers University. Darnton gives a brief history of the writings of Voltaire and their influence over philosophy, culture, and society.

[16] K. Collins, *John Wesley: A Theological Journey*, (Nashville, TN: Abingdon Press, 2003), 43–44.

[17] K. Collins, *John Wesley: A Theological Journey*, 260–61.

[18] B. Shelley, *Church History in Plain Language*, third edition, 369.

[19] Ibid., 369.

[20] For a fuller understanding of what the Global Leadership Summit does, it is best if the reader visits www.willowcreek.com/events/leadership. It is also important to understand that this is not an endorsement of or against the GLS. This is strictly for informational purposes. It illustrates the breadth

and depth of how leadership has become such an integral part of our society, for God's kingdom and in secular society.

[21] J. Kouzes and B. Posner, *The Leadership Challenge*, fifth edition (San Francisco, CA: The Leadership Challenge, 2010), 86.

[22] D. Elmer, *Cross-Cultural Communication* (Downers Grove, IL: IVP Academic, 2002), 89.

3

I Have a Theory

To this point, we have seen different levels of leadership as they have been presented through history, and most notably, biblical history. But we should not assume that we can completely understand why leaders act the way they do. To help in this endeavor means there must be deployment of certain theories to make sense out of what we perceive. It turns the how and what into the why.

Each theory and approach that is presented in this chapter should bring us a little closer to developing an understanding of some basic principles so that when we begin to look at different styles, there is a baseline in which we may adjust our own leadership. These theories and approaches should help in determining what drives thoughts, behaviors, attitudes, and motivations. As you read them, try and imagine how they relate to you and the way you lead.

Leader-Member Exchange Theory

Leader-member exchange theory, or LMX, focuses on the exchanges between leaders and followers.[1] But it also incorporates a dyadic relationship that moves into two categories known as the *inner group* and the *outer group*.[2] The dyadic relationships develop critical skills and emotions within the leader-follow dynamic that are necessary to maintain mutual growth and accomplishment. These skills and emotions include trust, reliability, dependability, and honesty, which characterize a high-quality relationship.[3] Each group's aim is to build on a noble exchange versus a sordid one. It is for the latter of these that LMX theory has gained criticism among scholars, however.

A major criticism involves the validity of LMX to give leaders any practical wisdom for building meaningful relationships. From a group perspective, critics say that it divides the inner and outer groups by promoting inequality and a hierarchal chasm instituted by favoritism.[4] Since LMX theory revolves around leader-group relationships, it seems at least plausible that this criticism is not completely unfounded. Nevertheless, there are positive attributes that may outweigh this criticism—especially with regard to godly purposes.

One of the important aspects of leadership is developing future leaders out of followers. This task becomes increasingly difficult with a larger follower base. This is precisely why LMX theory is important—it validates that the dyads formed in the inner group have a greater motivation to become leaders because the leader gives more attention to the inner group.[5] This does not mean that the outer group does not receive attention. It simply means they do not receive as much attention, which brings us full circle back to the main criticism.

In any case, LMX theory provides a reality check to understand the importance of inner and outer groups because it forces leaders to realize their capabilities and limitations. That is, the leader needs to know how many they can effectively teach to become future leaders and how many are willing to follow along with them. Stretching leadership too thin has the detriment of a lower-quality leadership. It also becomes a delicate balancing act to ensure that the outer group is not alienated because of the attentiveness of the inner group. It is very tempting to continue to support those who are willing to follow while ignoring those who are less involved. In this regard there is inequality, and this needs constant monitoring to ensure it does not happen or is corrected before it is too late. This brings into question the role of personality convergence and LMX theory because many assume that leaders garner inner groups because of personality similarities.

Unfortunately, studies differ on personality as an antecedent to LMX theory. Most studies demonstrate the similarities between followers and leaders and the draw of one personality to the other.[6] Nevertheless, the number of studies that differ is important enough to identify as inconclusive with regard to personality antecedents. This is good news for both leaders and followers because it demonstrates the reliance on the Holy Spirit as the antecedent to make LMX theory truly work. To illustrate LMX theory best, we now turn to the leader—Jesus.

Most have heard of Jesus's inner and outer group. The majority call this His inner circle of disciples—notably, Peter, James, and John. Upon examination we find that Jesus demonstrated LMX theory by developing multiple layers of followers. First, there were the twelve disciples whom Jesus taught more intimately and outside of the majority. But inside the twelve He had three others, as previously mentioned.

The book of Mark gives us three separate occasions that identify Peter, James, and John as guests to some of Jesus's special events. There was the invitation to Jairus's home to raise his dead daughter.[7] Then, there was Jesus's transfiguration on the mountain.[8] Finally, they accompanied Jesus to the garden of Gethsemane.[9] Each of these places had a special place within the gospel story. But why did those three get picked to be in Jesus's inner group? Jesus seemed to have a special purpose for the three of them and therefore gave them passage to privileged events. When we apply the principle of LMX theory, which states the inner group becomes more motivated because of the special attention received, the choosing of these three begins to take form. This is not to say that Jesus did not pay attention to the other nine, because clearly He did. It is to say, however, that Jesus developed certain attributes in Peter, James, and John that were not necessary for the others. This is what great leaders do. They identify the strengths of their followers and build upon them so they may take on bigger roles and responsibilities.

Peter was given the task of shepherding the church and bearing his cross.

> Jesus said, "Feed My sheep. I tell you the truth, when you were younger you dressed yourself and went where you wanted; but when you are old you will stretch out your hands, and someone else will dress you and lead you where you do not want to go." Jesus said this to indicate the kind of death by which Peter would glorify God. Then He said to him, "Follow Me." (John 21:17d–19)

James and John also had special tasks ahead of them. James would become the first apostle to be martyred.[10] John would go on to write five New Testament books and was quite possibly the last apostle to be martyred.

> "You do not know what you are asking," Jesus said to them. "Can you drink the cup I am going to drink?" "We can," they answered. Jesus said, "you will indeed drink from my cup …" (Matthew 20:22–23a)

Leaders have such a task of developing new leaders to take their place and if done right, to excel far beyond. But they also have the task of preparing others for difficult situations. LMX theory provides a view of when leaders pull certain followers in to give them a little more insight into what may lie ahead. Although we are not Jesus, we can lead like Jesus. We may not be able to predict what kind of hardships one might go through, but we can prepare them as much as possible.

Path-Goal Theory

The idea of path-goal theory is that leaders can significantly influence and inspire followers to achieve their goals by clearing obstacles in their path, clarifying the path, and rewarding goals as they are met.[11] While the theory demonstrates a strong coaching premise, it is regarded as a leadership theory that develops followers to achieve more. This is true in part because its developer, Robert House, posited that a leader's attitudes and behaviors drive motivation and satisfaction, thereby pushing followers to want to do more for leaders and thus inspiring leaders to continue motivating their followers.[12] It maintains a circular momentum that feeds both leader and follower. The circular momentum is based, further, on the identification of four distinct leadership styles found with those who practice path-goal theory.[13]

The first style is directive, which is non-authoritarian and nonpunitive, contrary to what the name may imply. It is directive because the leader shows propensity to guide the follower toward a certain goal or agenda. The directive leader enjoys clarifying instructions so that ambiguity is minimal and success is most achievable.[14]

The second style is supportive leadership. This type of leadership builds upon the psychological aspect of goal achievement by continually supporting the followers' goal attainment. It also produces social engagement and self-confidence through positive reinforcement.[15]

A third style is participative leadership behavior. Participative leadership behavior is important in path-goal theory because it allows for followers to be engaged in decision-making processes, and it encourages creativity of ideas. The participative leader calls upon followers to collect thoughts in order to empower collaborative thinking. This also produces a friendly social pressure among peers to achieve goals consistent with greater value to the follower.[16]

The fourth leadership style is achievement-oriented behavior. This leadership style is as the name implies. It heightens the standard of performance in followers, pushing them toward greater challenges.[17]

Each of these leadership behaviors is dependent upon the situation and the attitudes and behaviors of the followers. For example, if a follower has an *internal locus of control*—a tendency to try to control all events in his or her life—then a participative leadership style is appropriate. For followers with an *external locus of control*, who believe that external forces have control over events and circumstances, a directive style of leadership is most appropriate.[18] For the person who follows God, there is a mixture of both; on one hand God controls the circumstances but gives enough autonomy to make decisions freely. This indicates that God directs our paths, even removes obstacles at times, but also encourages us by being supportive, sets high standards as an achievement-oriented leader would, and participates fully with His adherents.

Some criticisms conclude that path-goal theory fails to fully explain the relationship between leader behavior and follower motivation and that the follower may become dependent on the leader.[19] For the follower of God, this is not a bad thing. But there is merit in these criticisms pertaining to the human leader-follower dyad.

> Therefore my dear friends, as you have always obeyed—not only in my presence, but now much more in my absence—continue to work out your salvation with fear and trembling, for it is God who works in you to will and to act according to His good purpose. (Philippians 2:12–13)

In the absence of a leader, such as the apostle Paul, it was absolutely possible for the Philippian church to fall into chaotic discord. Paul urged them in his absence to continue to rely on the Lord. It was easy for them when Paul was around because he could remind them. Now, he was gone and they had to rely on the leaders Paul had trained. More than this, however, they had to rely on God. The same is true today.

Pastors, for example, are leaders in local churches. Consider what happens when the pastor takes a vacation or a leave of absence. Some of the congregants cease to function to their fullest capacity in Christ. Part of the reason for this is because they have grown so dependent on the pastor to keep them walking upright that they have forgotten, or have never learned, to put their full trust in God to do so. In the God-to-person sense, path-goal theory is perfectly in tune; but in the person-to-person sense, it is not. For the former to be completely compatible, the follower must do their part and be assured God will do His. For the latter to be completely compatible, the leader must ensure that the follower does not become dependent and thereby incapacitated in the absence of the leader.

Behavioral Approach

It is appropriate to begin this section with the findings of Robert Blake and Jane Mouton. Although their contributions came more than a decade after the Ohio State University and the University of Michigan conducted research into the behavioral aspects of leadership, Blake and Mouton's Managerial Grid® (Later refined and adapted into the Leadership Grid® by Robert Blake and Anne McCanse) remains the best-known model of managerial behavior.[20] But to give credit to both universities, Blake and Mouton captured what first began as a quest to determine what behaviors leaders needed in order to address a variety of situations. The universities' findings ultimately delivered two basic motivators that defined leader behaviors: task-oriented leadership and relationship-oriented leadership.

Without becoming too technical, think of a graph that has five points plotted and when viewed resemble the five points on a gaming die (connecting the plots makes an X). Each plot represents a leadership behavior exhibited toward followers. The bottom (horizontal axis) of the graph represents concerns for productivity, and the side (vertical axis) of the graph represents concern for persons.

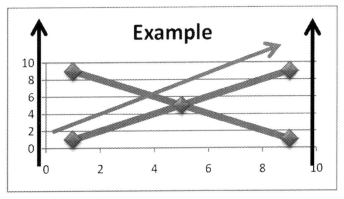

*This graph has been created by the author and is meant to be an example, for visual illustration purposes only, of the Managerial Grid® as developed by Blake and Mouton (1964) and revised as the Leadership Grid® by Blake and McCanse (1991). Expressed consent to use the actual copyrighted grids has not been obtained.

Looking at the graph, if the leader follows the horizontal axis, his or her main objective is production or results. If leaders follow the vertical axis, they are more relational in management style. The smaller the number on the graph, the less involved in that behavior the leader is. For example, if leaders have little interest in relational management and little interest in results, they most likely fall into the *Impoverished Management* (1,1) plot. When leaders have little interest in relational management and great interest in results, they fall into *Authority-Compliance Management* (9,1). The *Country Club Management* (1,9) suggests that the leader has greater interest in winning follower affection. *Middle-of-the-Road*

Management (5,5) identifies leaders as balanced, but not exceptional, at both behaviors. Each of these plots are assumptions into the leaders' dominant behaviors but also offer room to travel into situational, or backup, behaviors. The goal, however, is to find excellence in the balance of both behavioral tendencies.[21]

The red arrow on the graph indicates the desired direction of travel for the leadership behaviors. Ultimately, it is most desirable to achieve the 9,9 plot— *Team Management*. Team management suggests the leader is highly engaged in interpersonal relationships as well as accomplishing tasks. They have learned to bring teams together for greater productivity.[22]

The black arrows pointing up on the graph illustrate the upgraded edition of the Managerial Grid. These arrows indicate the situational nature that moves leaders from their dominant behavior(s) to their backup behavior(s) in order to benefit for personal gain. This is known as *Opportunism* and was developed by Blake and McCanse in 1991.[23]

Each aspect of the behavioral approach revolves around the person and the task. The entire premise is to demonstrate different levels of managerial expertise and to assume that leaders have a dominant and backup style of management. It also develops the opportunistic response that drives some leaders to take advantage of certain situations for personal gain. Nevertheless, the godly leader may benefit from studying behavioral theory in order to ascertain their own behavioral tendencies and either correct or improve upon them. To help determine what a successful godly leader looks like, we need look no further than Nehemiah.

Nehemiah is best known for rebuilding the wall around Jerusalem. But the credit is not for his personal rebuilding of the wall; rather, it is for his leadership to inspire others to rebuild the wall and his managerial skill in organization. There are right away two aspects of behavior at work—one is that Nehemiah had a kindred relationship with his fellow Jews and the second is that he had a task to accomplish.

The book of Nehemiah outlines the steps Nehemiah took to institute such a task. He petitioned the king of Persia to allow him to go to Jerusalem despite the possibility of death for showing sadness in front of the king. Nehemiah is also shown gathering people to inspect the ruined walls and gates and delegate appropriately. The monumental task of rebuilding a wall around the entire city of Jerusalem lasted only fifty-two days. This happened because Nehemiah demonstrated the target behavioral approach—that is, merging the relationship and task for maximum effectiveness and efficiency.

> So the wall was completed on the twenty-fifth of Elul, in fifty-two days. When all our enemies heard about this, all the surrounding nations were afraid and lost their self-confidence, because they realized that this work had been done with the help of our God. (Nehemiah 6:15–16)

Skills Approach

In the middle of the twentieth century, there was a great push to discover the identifiable skills of great executives. Organizations wanted to know how they could cultivate and foster these skills to produce the highest quality people. Instead of focusing on what good executives are, Robert Katz decided to focus on what good executives do.[24] Katz suggested that people were not necessarily born with certain skill sets that could be readily seen, but they could develop certain skills that could make them successful.[25] This began by defining administrators as those who directed activities of others and were charged with achieving certain objectives. Based on this generic administrator definition, three skills were identified: *technical skills, human skills, and conceptual skills.*[26]

Each skill makes up what is known as the *three-skill approach* and formed the base of future studies. It is also important to note that one skill is not necessarily more important than another, nor are they in any particular order. They do, however, demonstrate a greater need of possession based on the managerial level of the individual.

For example, technical skill is the proficiency demonstrated by an individual for any number of activities that is more important for the lower- and middle-level manager to possess and share. Human skill is very different from technical skill and requires knowledge about and the ability to work with other people. Human skill is equally important through all levels. Finally, conceptual skill is the ability to work with thoughts and ideas. Conceptual skill is used to create vision and strategy, which is mostly generated at upper-management levels.[27]

The three-skills approach was a precursor for other leadership researchers. It provided a framework for what was and is considered to be a practical and actionable take on leadership development via a theoretical approach to understanding how leadership is developed. For the most part, the three-skills approach was expanded to include a more robust outlook on what managers needed to have in their repertoire. It moved beyond the three skills previously mentioned to include five components: competencies, individual attributes, leadership outcomes, career experiences, and environmental influences.[28] The resulting research was termed *skills-based model.*[29]

The skills-based model was developed to look at the everyday leader, not just the exceptional leader.[30] This is why there are five components that reach a broad spectrum of attributes. Each component takes into account the attitudes, aptitudes, desires, and willingness of leaders to perform certain tasks or to lead others through them. But as appropriately pointed out as a possible weakness, the study conducted to come to these conclusions is based on a single militaristic environment that was looking for a better way to train military officers to handle different leadership scenarios.[31] This does not mean, however, that leaders outside the context of a military environment cannot examine these components and apply them to their environment. In this regard, it is possible to generalize the skills-based model.[32]

This brings us to the question of use, in particular, biblical use. That is to say, based on what we know about a skills approach, how do we determine this from the Bible? There is first a need for discernment in any biblical situation in which we may draw upon godly wisdom. Let us never forget that:

> If any of you lacks wisdom, he should
> ask God, who gives generously to all
> without finding fault, and it will be given
> to him. (James 1:5)

But we should also consider that this type of godly wisdom is for those who seek God's purposes. Nevertheless, it is within everyone's grasp. With this in mind, it makes it easier to ascertain the biblical use of the skills approach, especially when we make it easier upon ourselves to determine the three original areas in which all subsequent findings fall—human skill, technical skill, and conceptual skill.

To help with this, let us consider the actions of Solomon as he was presented with two prostitutes arguing over the motherhood of a baby.[33] We are first confronted with the "so what" position that identifies this particular scenario as more if a *Situational Leadership*® dilemma.[34] Although it may pertain, it is unimportant because we can still identify the skills present in the situation.

The human skills are most prevalent in Solomon's encounter. They are recognized first by the allowance of two prostitutes to bring a dispute before the king of Israel. Apparently there was enough interpersonal relationship between Solomon and the rest of the people that they did not fear bringing the dilemma to him. The technical skill is recognizable through the way in which the situation was handled. Solomon knew that if the product desired was to have the child delivered to both women, then he would see that it happened. As macabre as it sounds, it leads straight into the conceptual skill. This skill demonstrated the vision and strategy of Solomon to reveal the real mother. Instead of killing the baby and delivering two halves to each, he knew the real mother would rather give her child up then see it dead. The end result was:

> When all Israel heard the verdict the
> king had given, they held the king
> in awe, because they saw he had the
> wisdom from God to administer justice.
> (1 Kings 3:28)

Each of the theories and approaches gives a perspective on leadership and helps to identify strengths and weaknesses within the different styles. The chapters to come will identify further how different styles are presented and recognized. As we look at the styles, keep in mind how these theories and approaches are involved. How can you, as the reader and student, develop those styles through application of these theories and approaches to become a better, more-focused leader?

Chapter Notes

[1] A. Tzinerr and L. Barsheshet-Picker, "Authentic Management as a Moderator of the Relationship between the Congruence of Gender Role Identity-Gender Management Characteristics, and Leader-Member Exchange (LMX)," *Journal of Work and Organizational Psychology*, 30: 49–60, (2014).

[2] P. Northouse, *Leadership Theory and Practice*, seventh edition (Los Angeles: Sage, 2016), 138.

[3] A. Tzinerr and L. Barsheshet-Picker, "Authentic Management as a Moderator of the Relationship between the Congruence of Gender Role Identity-Gender Management Characteristics, and Leader-Member Exchange (LMX)," *Journal of Work and Organizational Psychology*, 30: 49–60, (2014).

[4] M. Hackman and C. Johnson, *Leadership: A Communication Perspective*, sixth edition (Long Grove, IL: Waveland, 2013), 94. Hackman and Johnson discuss the transformation of vertical dyad linkage (VDL) into LMX. They cover LMX theory with enough clarity to understand the importance of it and how it may be beneficial.

[5] P. Northouse, *Leadership Theory and Practice*, 145.

[6] G. Sears and R. Hackett, "The Influence of Role Definition and Affect in LMX: A Process Perspective on the Personality-LMX Relationship," *Journal of Occupational and Organizational Psychology*, 84: 544–64, (2011). Sears and Hackett cite multiple studies conducted identifying the personality relationship between leaders and followers in LMX theory. There are too many differing studies to be conclusive.

[7] Mark 5:35–43

[8] Mark 9:1–2

[9] Mark 14:32–33

[10] See Acts 12:2

[11] P. Northouse, 115.

[12] R. Vandegrift and J. Matusitz, "Path-goal theory: a successful Columbia Records story," *Journal of Human Behavior in the Social Environment*, 21, 352 (2011). Although Vandegrift and

Matusitz develop path-goal theory as it pertains to Columbia Records, they give a thorough definition and understanding of the theory.

[13] It should be noted that theories and styles are not the same. Theories encompass strategies and behaviors found within different styles of leadership. For example, path-goal theory is derived from the behavior leaders possess within, say, a directive style of leadership.

[14] R. House, "Path-goal theory of leadership: lessons, legacy, and reformulated theory," *Leadership Quarterly*, 7(3), 326, (1996).

[15] R. House, Path-goal theory of leadership, 326.

[16] R. House, 327.

[17] R. House, 327.

[18] P. Northouse, 119.

[19] P. Northouse, 124.

[20] P. Northouse, 74.

[21] R. Blake and J. Mouton, "An overview of the Grid®," *Training and Development Journal*, 29(5): 29–38 (1975).

[22] P. Northouse, 77. Peter Northouse gives a wonderful overview of all the plots contained on the Grid.

[23] P. Northouse, 78–79.

[24] R. Katz, "Skills of an effective administrator," *Harvard Business Review*, 52(5), p 91 (1974). This reprinting in Harvard Business Review is based on Robert Katz's original article of the same name published in 1955.

[25] R. Katz, Skills of an effective administrator, 1974, 92.

[26] R. Katz, 91.

[27] P. Northouse, 44–45.

[28] P. Northouse, 47.

[29] M. Mumford, S. Zaccaro, F. Harding, T. Jacobs, and E. Fleishman, "Leadership skills for a changing world: Solving complex social problems," *Leadership Quarterly*, 11(1), 11–35, (2000).

[30] M. Mumford, S. Zaccaro, M. Connelly, and M. Marks, "Leadership skills: conclusions and future directions," *Leadership Quarterly*, 11(1), 155–70, (2000).

[31] P. Northouse, 59.

[32] M. Mumford, S. Zaccaro, M. Connelly, et al.

[33] The entirety of the story can be found in 1 Kings 3:16–28.

[34] Situational Leadership® and Situational Leadership II (SLII®) were originally developed by Ken Blanchard and Paul Hersey. There is much to say on this approach, and it is widely used in organizational leadership training. While it is true that we may apply SLII® to this particular scenario, it is unnecessary to do so. SLII® has more than enough information to develop into its own section, but the concept itself is best used as an additive to other theories and styles because there is always a situation that dictates leadership response. For this reason, it will remain exempt from its own section but is recommended for the reader to explore.

4

Transformational and Transactional Leadership

Leadership styles come in varying shapes and sizes. It is important to note that one may not be superior to another in theory or practice; rather, it is the motivation behind the style that determines its worth. To help illustrate this, we begin by examining transformational and transactional leadership styles. Each has distinctive attributes and purposes, and it would be easy to think that transformational leadership is superior to transactional leadership because of how they are associated in case studies and various other literatures. This, then, brings us to the purpose of this chapter, and that is to present both leadership styles for what they are and how they compare and contrast. By the end of the chapter, there should be a better understanding of what each is and how they may benefit the leader and follower.

What's the Difference?

There is much to say about transformational leadership. In fact, James Kouzes and Barry Posner delivered a grand slam with leaders everywhere when they wrote *The Leadership Challenge*, which describes five practices of exemplary leaders as a model from the perspective of transformational leadership.[1] Those five principles include: model the way, inspire a shared vision, challenge the process, enable others to act, and encourage the heart.[2] But to understand a model such as this, we must first understand the origins of transformational leadership because this type of model outlines a set of behaviors and characteristics that stems from attitudes and desires of the leader. This is fitting since the origins of transformational leadership stem from studies in charismatic leadership.

It was in the early twentieth century that the term *charismatic* became identified with leadership at large. The early church thought of charismatic leadership as a God-ordained gift to certain church leaders. As time went, Christians began to see the value of God-given gifts in all His saints. But there were some, namely Max Weber, who brought the term over into the secular by describing people with certain gifts and radical visions that could inspire followers.[3] There was a pattern of behaviors that leadership scholars began noticing as well as a behavioral "transformation" that took place in followers. The result was that in the late 1970s James MacGregor Burns identified these behaviors as the first transformational approach to leadership.[4]

These behaviors—however scholars term them, whether visionary, empowering, creative, and the like—are what make transformational leadership such a strong and sought-after style. They focus on the idea of transforming a person based on positive and gifted leadership.

Transactional leadership, on the other hand, was considered by Burns to be the traditional style of leadership.[5] It is an exchange that takes place between leaders and followers. This exchange implies that leaders set goals for followers, and when followers satisfactorily complete the goals, rewards are given. If the goals are not completed, punishment becomes the reward.[6] For example, a high school teacher leads a student to learn a subject. If the student follows the teachers leading, then the student may receive an A for their work. If students do not follow the teacher's leading, they may receive an F. In either case, a letter grade is the reward of the transaction between the teacher and the student. In a sense there is a *quid pro quo* attitude between the leader and follower with transactional leadership that has potential to elicit less of a relationship that is so often desired with regard to leadership.

Although the difference may seem cut and dried, they can be hard to identify when the leader is faced with performing one or the other. That is, leaders may think they are transforming a follower when, in effect, they are really soliciting an exchange. Sometimes this completely rests on the follower and their attitude toward the leader, but it is also rests on the leader for failing to recognize what is happening too. Of course, there are times when the followers think they are involved in a transactional relationship when the leader is very involved in transforming them. For further illustration, let us consider Moses again.

As stated in the first chapter, Moses was called by God for a very specific purpose; he was to speak to Pharaoh about the oppression of God's people. At every step in the beginning Moses was unsure and uneasy. He questioned God, and God answered in kind exactly what Moses was to do. God led Moses through a series of transactions to demonstrate His power.[7] God is such a master at leadership that Moses did not realize what was happening to him. As we look to the end of Moses's life, there is a distinctly different person than the one who was afraid to even speak.

> Then Moses summoned Joshua and said to him in the presence of all Israel, "Be strong and courageous, for you must go with this people into the land the that the Lord swore to their forefathers to give them, and you must divide it among them as their inheritance. The Lord Himself goes before you and will be with you; He will never leave you or forsake you. Do not be afraid; do not be discouraged." (Deuteronomy 31:7–8)

There is a vast difference between what originally transpired between God and Moses to where Moses ended. His entire demeanor was transformed into a godly person who was speaking before the nation Israel and encouraging the next leader to take courage, knowing that God goes before them.

Is One Better Than the Other?

Thus far the differences in transformational leadership and transactional leadership have been quite distinguishable. The ambiguity is relevant only to the indistinguishable motives held by either the leader or the follower. But there is now the question as to which is better. Literature on the subject has given transformational leadership more praise than transactional; however, does this make it better?

One study indicated that transformational leadership focuses on exerted influence over the follower, which incites intellectual stimulation and thereby goal attainment. This same study also suggests that transactional leadership is based upon competitive achievement, which does not promote a team environment, nor does it encourage intellectual stimulation outside of one's own desire for reward. Nevertheless, this study's findings indicated that while transformational leadership styles promoted mastery of goals within a broad scope of team environment, transactional leadership promoted the adoption of performance goals on the individual level, concluding that organizations should adapt both styles to raise the collective and individual performance of an organization.[8]

This study is not unique and serves the purpose of identifying the answer to the question: Is one better than the other? It should be noted, however, that the way each style is defined plays an integral role in how they are used. Transformational leaders are thought to stimulate thinking through immediate problem solving and are actively engaged in developing followers to their full potential. Transactional leaders are thought to be passive until problems arise and offer contingent awards only as necessary.[9] The caveat to this dilemma is contained in the previous section, and the introduction of this one, which states it depends upon the motivations of both the leader and follower to determine not necessarily which is better, but which is appropriate. This leads us to examine motivation as it pertains to these leadership styles, or at least how the styles change to fit motivation.

Ultimately, transactional leadership produces an exchange between the leader and follower that can be considered motivated by positive or negative intentions. Transformational leadership, on the other hand, takes on a different role altogether, though it can build off transactional leadership. Both can have positive and negative effects on the follower provided the motives. When leaders have malicious intent for personal gain, they have entered into what is known as false leadership or *pseudotransactional* and *pseudotransformational* leadership.

One of the best depictions of this is the actions and leadership of Adolf Hitler and Saddam Hussein, who transformed followers and exchanged rewards with followers in a negative way.[10] Of course, there is a convincing argument made that these pseudo-leaders are not really leaders at all; rather, they cease to merit the privilege of being identified as leaders and deserve titles such as tyrant and despot for their self-consumed egos and warped morals.[11] How this translates to Christians should be of utmost concern. In other words, Christian leaders need to be on the lookout for these types of behaviors and guard against them in the church. Too many churches and denominations have risen, collided, and fallen at the hand of pseudo-leadership. It seems appropriate to mention Satan as this digression ends to demonstrate what pseudo-leadership looks like.

Right away there is the thought of Satan's encounter with Jesus in Matthew 4.[12] Anyone who knows Jesus knows this story almost seems comical. Nevertheless, this story allows the student to understand the true power of God. It shows His power because of the transaction that was offered by Satan and rejected by Jesus. The godly person understands Satan's agenda is contrary to God and therefore demonstrates a pseudo-leadership style. His motives are such that he offers Jesus earthly dominion in trade for worship. Imagine the implications if this transaction had taken place; imagine the transformation of character under Satan's pseudo-leadership!

> Be alert and of sober mind. Your enemy
> the devil prowls around like a roaring lion
> looking for someone to devour. (1 Peter 5:8)

One can argue that transformational leadership is better than transactional leadership, but the truth is they work best when implemented together. It seems appropriate to label it as *T and T Leadership* because it truly is an explosive combination. What determines their worth and power are the motivations of the leader and the willingness of the follower. Knowing when to capitalize on each is mostly understood by more experienced leaders. However, many have demonstrated each of these leadership styles without realizing it. Experienced leaders recognize when they are conducting a transaction and when they are leading for transformation. But they also know how to conduct both in a godly manner.

Leadership for Effective Change

Surmising that each has its purpose and that they are best used interdependently, we may still conclude that there are some specific times in which they may stand alone. The best example of this involves a fear that is often unnecessary, and that is change. It mustn't be fearful, however. On the contrary, it should be exciting and forward-thinking. Change, for any organization, can be a much-needed step in a much-needed direction. But change is best reserved for transformational leadership.

It is unnecessary to revisit our study of transformational leadership traits. What is important is taking those traits and applying them to lead through change. One way to do this is by understanding that transformational leaders are disinterested in gaining power or choosing to be a leader; rather, the deepest desire is to effect change itself.[13] Suffice it to say that a leader who really wants transformational change will willingly demonstrate what that looks like.

For example, Jesus is considered the kind of leader who demonstrates what it means to be a transformational leader. After all, He did dedicate His life and ministry to teaching and doing what He desired others to do.

> In my former book, O Theophilus, I wrote about all that Jesus began to do and teach until the day that He was taken up to heaven, after giving instructions through the Holy Spirit to the apostles He had chosen. (Acts 1:1–2)

Thinking back on what has been covered in this chapter, it is clear this passage of Scripture outlines what has been discovered according to transformational and transactional leadership. There are three key words to demonstrate this: do, teach, and instructions. These words identify Jesus's T and T style of leadership in actionable terms; in other words, He proved what He taught by living the lifestyle He promoted and told the others to do it too. There is one final element here that allows the transformation to be complete—the Holy Spirit.

The apostle Paul knew that for any change to happen in the Christian life, there had to be a transformation of people's thought processes. His masterful work addressed to the Romans clarified this in 12:2 by his admission that in order to know what God's will is, there must be a mind transformation that moves in a different direction than the world's. The only entity that could make such a mind-transforming change to know God's will is the Holy Spirit working inside each person. This is where individual change comes from. This is also how leaders and followers effect change for the masses.

Chapter Notes

[1] J. Kouzes and B. Posner, *The Leadership Challenge*, fifth edition (San Francisco: Wiley, 2012). Kouzes and Posner developed their five principles based on over thirteen hundred interviews of middle and senior managers in public and private sectors. Their results identify a model of transformational style and are very useful in practice.

[2] J. Kouzes and B. Posner, *The Leadership Challenge*, 15.

[3] M. Hackman and C. Johnson, *Leadership: A Communication Perspective*, sixth edition (Long Grove, IL: Waveland, 2013), 121.

[4] J. Burns, *Leadership* (New York: Harper & Row, 1978). James Burns's original literature of the same name first came out in 1973.

[5] M. Hackman and C. Johnson, *Leadership*, 100.

[6] A. Rodrigues and M. Ferreira, "The impact of transactional and transformational leadership style on organizational citizenship behavior," *Psico-USF, 20*(3): 493–504, (2015).

[7] See Exodus 4:1–9. God continually demonstrates His power to Moses who seemed skeptical. This is indicative of a transactional relationship between God and Moses.

[8] M. Hamstra, N. Yperen, B. Wisse, and K. Sassenberg, "Transformational and transactional leadership and followers' achievement goals," *Journal of Business Psychology, 29*: 413–25, (2014). The authors interviewed and studied 449 followers of 120 leaders from diverse organizations. The participants were asked to fill out a questionnaire regarding their leader's style of leadership and their achievement goals.

[9] B. Avolio and B. Bass, *Developing Potential Across a Full Range of Leadership™: Cases on Transactional and Transformational Leadership* (Mahwah, NJ: LEA Publishers, 2002).

[10] P. Northouse, *Leadership Theory and Practice*, seventh edition (Los Angeles, CA: Sage, 2016), p. 163.

[11] B. Bass and R. Riggio, *Transformational Leadership*, second edition (Mahwah, New Jersey: LEA Publishers, 2006). Source contained in the foreword written by James Burns.

[12] See Matthew 4:1–11.

[13] W. Burke, *Organization Change Theory and Practice*, fourth edition (Los Angeles, CA: Sage, 2014), 293.

5

Authentic Leadership

Life circumstances have a way of developing our character. As discussed earlier, we often choose to lead someone based on past learned experience. There are times when what we go through individually becomes our passion to lead others collectively. There can be ups and downs to this thought process, but it also offers an unparalleled efficacy that drives leaders to pursue great things for followers. The flip side of this is when the passion of the leader muddles the development of the follower and results in a stifling effect. The problem, however, is that there is no one defining quality of authentic leadership. There are differing yet interwoven definitions of authentic leadership that must be considered before anyone can definitively identify authentic leadership.

The following should help put authentic leadership into perspective. We will discuss the psychological side as well as the practical. We will engage the characteristics that represent an authentic style and how they apply in developing not only followers but leaders as well. By the end of this chapter, there should be a clear understanding of the difference between authenticity and sincerity. That is to say, authentic leadership is not sincere leadership because one's sincerity does not always account for one's internal character.[1]

What Is It?

Authentic leadership is based on two pretenses: an authentic person and a level of efficacy that catapults the authentic leader beyond other leaders.[2] The reason this seems possible is because most believe that authentic leaders are true to themselves and their beliefs, which enables them to build trust among others and motivate people in deeper ways.[3] When followers see leaders as authentic, they tend to open up more than when they see them as misleading or even fake. For example, a manager who consistently pushes his employees out of the office to spend time with their family may seem like a caring leader. But if that manager is consistently staying late and avoiding his or her own family, then why should an employee approach him or her with personal family concerns? The authentic leader will have a desire to demonstrate a healthy work-life balance if family time is of real value to him or her. Arguments can be made that the family is prized for both, but followers have the final say in the matter because they respond to the leader based on what the leader reveals to them.

This illustration helps with the understanding of how authentic leadership works. It lets followers know that no matter how well-intentioned the leaders, they must indicate their true selves by demonstrating their true self. Knowing this indicates that one may break down authentic leadership into two basic approaches: practical and theoretical. The practical approach is based on life experiences, while the theoretical approach is based on social science research.[4] Let's first look at the practical approach.

Bill George was a longtime corporate executive who began researching what characteristics authentic leadership held. After interviewing more than one hundred executives, George mapped out five characteristics that authentic leaders possess: 1) an understanding of their purpose, 2) strong values of the right thing to do, 3) the ability to establish trusting relationships with others, 4) the ability to demonstrate self-discipline and act on their values, 5) and passion about their mission.[5] These characteristics identify the practical approach to authentic leadership because they are attainable for anyone who has a desire to serve others. This is important because it implies the authentic leader is a positive leader, which separates it from the reality that negative and malicious people can be authentic.

The theoretical approach is based on the empirical research of those who seem to demonstrate authentic leadership. The difficulty with the theoretical approach is defining the characteristics of authentic leadership. One might think that the characteristics are the same as those found in the practical approach, but this is not the case. Instead, the theoretical approach focuses on the construct and development of the positive psychological capacities and moral reasoning.[6] These are the underlying measures of how authentic leadership works. To be fair, the theoretical approach introduces a practical awareness to effective development of authentic leadership. That is to say researchers have identified four areas from theoretical research used to examine and develop a practical outcome: *self-awareness, relational transparency, internalized moral perspective,* and *balanced processing.*[7] Instead of diving into defining what each of these is, it is more prudent to find a commonality between the practical and theoretical approaches.

Notice that each focuses on the positive attributes of an individual. These positive attributes are at the center of what defines authentic leadership. In reality, the practical and theoretical approaches are overlapping.

Figure 5.1 Commonalities between Practical and Theoretical Approaches to Authentic Leadership

Practical	Theoretical	Commonality
Understanding of purpose; self-discipline and ability to act on values; passion toward mission	Self-awareness; balanced processing	Ability to understand own capabilities and limitations while maintaining sensitivity to others' perspectives
Strong values of the right thing to do; passion toward mission	Internalized moral perspective; balanced processing	Heart is full but not unaware of how actions affect others, especially in an ethical manner and not for self-gain

Establish trusting relationships; passion toward mission	Relational transparency; balanced processing	Allows others to understand them by being open and honest without letting this rule decisions or actions

Sources: B. George and P. Sims, *True North: Discover Your Authentic Leadership*, (San Francisco: Jossey-Bass, 2007) & F. Walumbwa, B. Avolio, W. Gardner, T. Wernsing, and S. Peterson, Authentic Leadership: Development and Validation of a Theory-Based Measure, *Journal of Management*, 34 (1), 2008.

Note: The commonalities between both sources are the author's findings and may not represent the sources.

Figure 5.1 demonstrates the relationship between the two approaches in a way that helps leaders understand how they can examine and apply their own authentic leadership. And as stated in the beginning of the chapter, authentic leadership is something that is often learned through life experience and circumstance. Events in our lives help to shape and mold us, and when we maintain transparency through leading, followers are more apt to be inspired by us. For example, think about an episode when you explained past experiences to demonstrate to others that you understood what they might be going through. This is transparency. In the same way, we should not pretend that we know exactly how to deal with every situation. New territory should be addressed as such and not postured as if we are all-knowing experts. This remains authentic leadership when we are able to explain to our followers that we may not have a firm grasp on their current circumstances, but we still pour our compassion and heart into it anyway. That is why, as Christian leaders, we must know God's word. His word is where we find how to extrapolate information in order to best help others.

> IFor My thoughts are not your thoughts, nor are your ways My ways," says the LORD. "For as the heavens are higher than the earth, so are My ways higher than your ways, and My thoughts than your thoughts. For as the rain comes down, and the snow from heaven, and do not return there, but water the earth, and make it bring forth and bud, that it may give seed to the sower, and bread to the eater, so shall My word be that goes forth from My mouth; it shall not return to Me void, but it shall accomplish what I please, and it shall prosper for the thing which I sent it." (Isaiah 55:8–11 NKJV)

Authentic biblical leaders realize the gravity of this and act accordingly. The authentic leader will search the Scriptures for understanding and wisdom in situations not immediately known.

Consider the apostle Paul as an authentic leader. When he wrote his final letters, he did so with a wise and tested heart. He called upon his past experiences to let Timothy know the importance of and difficulties in pastoral work. Paul was transparent, he was caring, he was reasonable, and he was aware of his capabilities and limitations. To cover all bases, Paul knew it was necessary to recall humankind's instruction book for life.

> All Scripture is God-breathed and is
> useful for teaching, rebuking, correcting
> and training in righteousness, so that
> the servant of God may be thoroughly
> equipped for every good work. (2 Timothy
> 3:16–17)

For the Christian leader, being authentic wins the favor of both God and people.

Defining Values

Since so much of authentic leadership relies on values-based leading, it is appropriate to define how they pertain, why they are important, and which to choose. As J. Oswald Sanders points out, "Not every Christian is called to major leadership in the church, but every Christian is a leader, for we all influence others. All of us should strive to improve our leadership skills."[8] In order for Christian leaders to lead, they must know where their values come from and what they are. In the same way, our values guide our commitment. Values are the center for the decisions we make, the judgments we act upon, and how we respond to others. Any option that runs contrary to our values is usually not acted upon, and if they are, they are done out of compliance rather than commitment.[9]

Ken Blanchard suggests that values retain the essence of leadership and that any leader should not focus on more than a few values.[10] This idea has merit because it allows the leader to intentionally develop a

few values earnestly instead of getting bogged down
with too many values that are underdeveloped. This does
not mean that leaders cannot have many values; it simply
means they should hone a few at a time. Followers need
to know their leaders are consistent. If a leader tries to
master too many values at once, it may cause burnout
for both the leader and follower, not to mention the lack
of focal development on their values.

Part of the difficulty with this is knowing which
values should be focused on for leadership purposes.
To be sure, this truly cannot be answered by anyone
but the leader. Nevertheless, according to the World
Council of Churches, there are several values to choose
from, including wisdom, integrity, responsibility, justice,
freedom, reliability, modesty, and courage just to name
a few.[11] This should not surprise the Christian leader
because they embody the teachings of the Bible. From
a very early age, the Bible speaks about gaining godly
values to keep with the ways of God.

> Start children off in the way they should
> go, and when they are old they will not
> turn from it. (Proverbs 22:6)

Should this Scripture also not hold true with
leadership? The idea of children is that someone must
train and lead them into adulthood. The same is true
for followers; that is, they must be led into leadership
positions. Teach a child to have ungodly values and
the result could be disastrous. The same holds true to
followers. Too many followers glean ungodly values

from leaders even if that was never the intent. Christian leaders need to be cognizant of who surrounds them because watching eyes and listening ears may be prepared to accept what they see and hear. This is what being an authentic leader is about, however. It is about being genuine in a godly manner no matter who is near. This is only done by ingraining God and His word on our hearts. The first part of the *Shema* declares this for every believer and was meant to be recited as an affirmation of life.

> Hear, O Israel, The LORD our God, the LORD is one. Love the LORD your God with all your heart and with all your soul and with all your strength. These commandments that I give you today are to be on your hearts. Impress them on your children. Talk about them when you sit at home and when you walk along the road, when you lie down and when you get up. Tie them as symbols on your hands and bind them on your foreheads. Write them on the doorframes of your houses and on your gates. (Deuteronomy 6:4–9)
>
> That is the beginning of true authentic leadership.

Putting It Together

Once values are determined and practiced and once godly understanding is evident, the leader must be able to combine their character with their reputation. We should never try to fool ourselves in thinking that these two cannot become estranged from one another. Too many Christian leaders have fallen at the hands of pride and arrogance. This means that the authentic leader, in order to exemplify godly values and virtues, must show all signs of humility.

Humility is the very attribute that keeps an authentic leader authentic. Without humility, the authentic leader walks a dangerous line of being unauthentic in terms of positivity and marrying character and reputation. Leaders should strive to develop such a humble attitude that they have no choice but to, as discussed earlier, exhibit self-discipline, relational transparency, balanced processing, passion toward their mission, and knowing and adhering to their godly values.

Kouzes and Posner state, "Humility is the only way to resolve the conflicts and contradictions of leadership."[12] They also suggest that humility is the antidote to hubris, which, when employed, becomes a powerful tool to be authentic.[13] Leaders who demonstrate humility will know they cannot do everything themselves. They must rely on others because they demonstrate their humanity.

The same is true for each Christian leader. In fact, the apostle Paul knew that he did not have the stamina or ability to lead anyone without the strength of Christ. He knew that in every situation he must call on Christ to usher him through. Paul declares to the Philippians that he has learned to be content in all things because of the strength Christ gives him. He declares that he has tasted abundance and poverty, he tasted wellness and pain, and he has been full and hungry.

> I can do all things through Christ who strengthens me. (Philippians 4:13 NKJV)

Leaders, it is Christ who gives us the strength to lead. It is Christ who gives us the strength to be humble. It is Christ who leads us. And if ever there was an authentic leader, it is Christ. Pursue Christ in earnest to show others what an authentic leader is.

Chapter Notes

[1] A. Chan, S. Hannah, and W. Gardner, "Veritable Authentic Leadership: Emergence, Functioning, and Impacts," in *Authentic Leadership Theory and Practice: Origin, Effects, and Development*, ed. B. Avolio, W. Gardner, and F. Walumbwa, from *Monographs in Leadership and Management*, vol. 3, edited by J. Hunt (San Diego, CA: Elsevier, 2005), 6.

[2] A. Chan, S. Hannah, and W. Gardner, "Veritable Authentic Leadership: Emergence, Functioning, and Impacts," 4.

[3] B. George and P. Sims, *True North: Discover Your Authentic Leadership* (San Francisco, CA: Jossey-Bass, 2007), xxxi.

[4] P. Northouse, *Leadership Theory and Practice*, seventh edition (Los Angeles, CA: Sage, 2016), 197.

[5] P. Northouse, *Leadership*, 197 as referenced in B. George, *Authentic Leadership: Rediscovering the Secrets to Building Lasting Value* (San Francisco, CA: Jossey-Bass, 2003).

6   F. Walumbwa, B. Avolio, W. Gardner, T. Wernsing, and S. Peterson, "Authentic Leadership: Development and Validation of a Theory-Based Measure," *Journal of Management*, 34(1): 89–126 (2008).

7   F. Walumbwa, et al, "Authentic Leadership: Development and Validation of a Theory-Based Measure," *Journal of Management*, 34 (1): 120–21 (2008).

8   J. O. Sanders, *Spiritual Leadership: Principles of Excellence for Every Believer* (Chicago: Moody Publishers, 2007), 109.

9   J. Kouzes and B. Posner, *The Leadership Challenge*, fifth edition (San Francisco, CA: The Leadership Challenge, 2010), 49.

10 K. Blanchard, *Leading at a Higher Level*, Revised (Upper Saddle River, NJ: FT Press, 2010), 295.

11 O. Ike, "Core Values for Responsible Leadership: The Relevance of Ethics for Religion and Development," *The Ecumenical Review*, 68(4): 463–71 (2017).

12 J. Kouzes and B. Posner, *The Leadership Challenge*, fifth edition (San Francisco: The Leadership Challenge, 2010), 340.

13 J. Kouzes and B. Posner, *The Leadership Challenge*, 341.

6

Servant Leadership

For the Christian leader, no other leadership style takes center stage as servant leadership does. Christian leaders recognize that Jesus had a ministry of service. In fact the entire gospel according to Mark revolves around the central statement found in the tenth chapter:

> For even the Son of Man did come to be
> served, but to serve, and give His life as
> a ransom for many. (Mark 10:45)

The interesting part about this is that servant leadership was not considered a mainstream leadership style until the 1970s. It seems strange that a central theme, such as found in the book of Mark, which exclaims a servant leadership style, was not a viable leadership style option until some two thousand years later. What may be even more interesting is the unique nature that servant leadership takes. It is, as some might call, paradoxical because it is counter-intuitive to what one may think of when thinking of leadership.[1] In fact, Robert Greenleaf, whose seminal work brought servant leadership to light, said that best leaders were those who served and that real leaders were servants.[2] In order to completely grasp servant leadership, however, there need be an understanding of what it is.

What It Isn't and What It Is

The first part is to define what servant leadership is not so that we can understand what it is. This includes declaring that without the ten characteristics of servant leadership, it is not really servant leadership. We shall see those characteristics in more detail later. For now, suffice it to say that a servant leader is not simply a servant. Instead, servant leaders are those who puts others' needs before their own in order to develop them.[3] If one is only content to serve, there is no fault in that. Nevertheless, it does not necessarily make them a leader in sense of the word. That is unless it inspires others to action as well.

Greenleaf believed that the servant leader served others out of love.[4] This sentiment means that love is a prerequisite for servant leadership. In other words, if one does not serve out of love with intention to inspire others to action and has no need of putting others first, rather they serve out of obligation or duty, then they are not practicing servant leadership. The apostle Paul said in a letter to the Corinthians:

And now these three remain: faith, hope,
and love. But the greatest of these is love.
(1 Corinthians 13:13)

Greenleaf was heavily influenced by Methodist
and Quaker thought when it came to love and service.
Although he did not necessarily agree with every aspect
of each sect, he did believe that all people have the
ability to harness the light that is inside them and use
this for service of leadership.[5] No matter the theological
implications, which Greenleaf was not fanatic about
anyway (in fact, he was more concerned about practice
than thought, which is why he had no real desire for
theological ideas), the light that he agreed was inside
each person to demonstrate good character was the light
of God even if unknown to the individual. This light was
the concrete idea, according to Greenleaf, of love.

No matter Greenleaf's individual philosophy, one
thing is agreed upon for students of servant leadership—
that is, the central theme revolves around love. God sent
His Son to the world out of love. Jesus Christ served
others out of love. In the process of serving others out
of love, He led them, and leads us, in a very unique and
special way. This demonstrates that servant leadership
is the embodiment of God's love toward humankind.[6]
Leaders in the church should recognize the importance
of love when it comes to leading and how this impacts
their ability to lead in a servant manner rather than a
self-serving manner.

Ken Blanchard and Phil Hodges state that Jesus
used His time and efforts on earth to model what service

to others should look like and how to execute servant leadership in such a way that it is actually paving the way for future leaders. They go on to state that if people are to be successful servant leaders, then they must consider their current position on loan and a placeholder for the next leader.[7] This idea has no room for the self-serving leader because it suggests leaders are not in their position for personal gain; it suggests they are in their position for others to gain. Going back to the concept of love, it is difficult to argue, if not impossible, that one who is self-serving has more love for themselves than for others. The ideals of being self-serving are contrary to the ideals of servant leadership.

Defining Characteristics

There have been ten characteristics identified from Greenleaf's work. It is important to note, however, that these ten characteristics were not identified by Greenleaf himself. These are observations from another who gleaned the essence of what Greenleaf taught and theorized, and they have since become representative of Greenleaf's work.[8]

Greenleaf's seminal essay developed an idealistic approach to social responsibility with regard to leaders' roles within organizations. The result is a leader who transforms followers through a long-term commitment of positivity and service for a better society.[9] The identified steps to get there were outlined as follows: *listening, empathy, healing, awareness, persuasion, conceptualization, foresight, stewardship, commitment to the growth of people, and building community.* It is important to look at each characteristic in order to truly understand how they apply.

Listening is a skill that is best learned through discipline. That is to say that the servant leader has interest in listening before they offer speech in order to understand the follower's perspective.[10] If ever there was a godly principle, it is this; however, it is the one that also eludes our judgment at times.

> My dear brothers and sisters take note of this: Everyone should be quick to listen, slow to speak and slow to become angry, because human anger does not produce the righteousness that God desires. (James 1:19-20)

This sums up the essence of listening as a servant leader. Anger is often a product due to lack of listening, because understanding has not been reached. And it should be noted that anger may fester and grow resentment. It should also be noted that anger in a leader-follower relationship has no partiality. Both parties are susceptible to anger, and the servant leadership dynamic becomes threatened when anger is presented because of a lack of listening on the leader's part.

Empathy may be described as the ability to internalize and emotionally attach to another's sentiments, views, or emotional state. According to both Spears and Northouse, when leaders empathize with followers, it makes them feel unique.[11] It does this because followers feel that the leader values them as individuals. In no less than three places, the Bible speaks of spiritual gifts (Romans 12:1–8; 1 Corinthians 12:1–11; Ephesians 4:11). The servant leader recognizes these gifts as something special and connects with the individual in order to encourage them to carry their gifts out. In this way, the follower does indeed feel unique within the church.

> For we do not have a High Priest who is unable to empathize with our weaknesses, but we have one who has been tempted in every way, just as we are—yet He did not sin. (Hebrews 4:15)

Healing, with regard to the servant leader, is the desire to make their followers whole and complete. Greenleaf believed that servant leaders should be able to recognize and help others heal from past hurts and in the process, often become healed from something themselves.[12] The tendency might be to conclude that this is simply ministering to others, and that would not be a wrong perspective. From a psychological perspective, healing might be considered compassion, which is a logical progression from empathy.[13] Again, this is not incorrect. Servant leaders want to immerse themselves in their followers' hurts to help them move forward.

> Jesus said to them, "It is not the healthy who need a doctor, but the sick. I have not come to call the righteous, but the sinners." (Mark 2:17)

In this passage, Jesus is clearly immersing Himself with those who are in need of ultimate healing. He understands the importance of diagnosing hurts and the impact healing has on followers. The same is true for all servant leaders—they see the value in healing others.

Awareness is the characteristic of being sober and awake. It allows the leader to understand more accurately issues that involve ethics and values.[14] Much of this comes from leaders being aware of not only themselves but of their surroundings that are impacted by physical, social, and political environments.[15] This enables leaders to respond to followers' needs based on what is happening in their inner and outer sphere of influences. It also enables leaders to open a dialogue with their followers to discuss the impact of what is happening in and around them. For the Christian servant leader, it also means being aware of what spiritual powers are at work against developing their leader-follower relationship and ultimately against God's work. It is always appropriate to remind ourselves:

> Be alert and of sober mind. Your enemy
> the devil prowls around like a roaring lion
> looking for someone to devour. (1 Peter 5:8)

Persuasion is an attribute that emphasizes thought-provoking and clearly defined commentary over positional authority. In other words, the servant leader seeks to give compelling detail rather than coerce their followers into something.[16] Perhaps it was Greenleaf's affiliation with the Religious Society of Friends

(Quakers) and their consistent congregational meetings that had an impact on his inclusion of this characteristic. After all, Greenleaf's admiration of the way the Quakers conducted meetings and business was widely known because he saw it as serving the thoughts and ideas of others rather than one or a few making decisions for all.[17] The idea of persuasion, regarding servant leadership, is to be in direct contradiction to authoritarian rule and more in partnership with a democratic leadership. It allows followers to make informed decisions based the leader's guidance.

When Paul stood in front of the philosophers at the Areopagus, he spoke with clarity of speech and great detail. He knew that he was in the midst of people who did nothing but speak about ideas and philosophies, so Paul made it a point to persuade these people as he led them to Christ.[18] The importance of service can be seen in Paul's service to God and to the people surrounding him. Moreover, servant leadership is seen in the way in which Paul used persuasive speech to allow the people of the Areopagus to come to a conclusion of their own.

Conceptualization is the characteristic that describes a servant leader's ability to visualize organizational goals and ideas. It is a look beyond the day-to-day operations; it looks to future events as they are expected to unfold.[19] Conceptualization often deals in abstract visions of what could and should be based on where the organization as a whole wants to be. Conceptualization is a way to serve followers by keeping them on track to pursue worthy goals. In the same way, it gives followers a clear sense of purpose when it is a noble and worthy goal.[20] Kouzes and Posner state it this way: "You need to describe a compelling image of what the future could be like when people join together in a common cause."[21] When leaders and followers share a vision, a common goal, it places each at the service of the other because they must reach it together.

Jesus taught the disciples to be "fishers of men" because His conceptualization was to change the world.[22] Jesus spent the next few years living out and serving based on His vision of the future for them and everyone else. The disciples apparently carried this vision forward based on what others were saying about them as demonstrated by an angry mob in Thessalonica as they searched for Paul and Silas.

> But when they did not find them, they dragged Jason and some brethren to the rulers of the city, crying out, 'These who have turned the world upside have come here too." (Acts 17:6 NKJV)

Paul and Jason may have not walked with Jesus during His ministry, but one thing is certain: Christ's principle of conceptualization was demonstrated and passed on to others!

Foresight is described as the servant leadership characteristic that the leader knows what is going to happen based on current ethical happenings.[23] It is the leader's responsibility to demonstrate a reasonable understanding of what will happen when certain actions are taken. Foresight enables the leader to plan for the future because of the present.[24] It differs from conceptualization because it does not deal in the idealistic; it deals in the direct results of current events.

God's word promises us that the things we go through now will help shape us in the future. That is to say that when hard times fall upon us, we will grow stronger, more resilient as we remain faithful to Him. The book of James tells us this most plainly:

> Consider it pure joy my brothers and sisters, when you face trials of many kinds, because you know that testing of your faith produces perseverance. Let perseverance finish its work so that you may be pure and complete, not lacking anything. (James 1:2–4)

The key word here is *consider*. Consider means to literally think into the future about the outcome of your circumstance. This is what servant leaders do. They think into the future of the outcome of what they and their followers are currently going through. The servant leader sees it as an obligation to prepare their followers for the future.

Stewardship is when the servant leader assumes responsibility for the organizational administration of trust for the greater good.[25] In other words, servant leaders hold to the accountability they have to ensure that each follower is taken care of through their own cognition of oversight.

> Be shepherds of God's flock that is
> under your care, watching over them—
> not because you must, but because you
> are willing, as God wants you to be; not
> pursuing dishonest gain, but eager to
> serve; not lording it over those entrusted
> to you, but being examples to the flock.
> (1 Peter 5:2–3)

Peter's exhortation to fellow elders is to care for those they have been entrusted with. The same is true for the servant leader. The servant leader does what is right for the sake of all, watching diligently and honestly.

Commitment to the growth of people is at the very core of servant leadership. This characteristic is arguably what makes this leadership style unique. The reason is because it puts much emphasis on personally and professionally developing individuals to become more contributable to society and better leaders overall. Servant leaders find personal commitment to each person—they take a personal interest in their lives.[26]

Consider the time Priscilla and Aquila spent with Apollos. The couple heard Apollos speak about Jesus and decided he was very educated in the Scriptures, yet he seemed to be lacking in some areas. Priscilla and Aquila recognized an opportunity to help Apollos understand God's word more accurately. They exercised servant leadership by taking a personal interest in Apollos by bringing him into their home. They instructed him in such a way that his personal and professional life was enhanced.[27]

Building community is the final characteristic of servant leadership. It is the desire for likeminded people to gather together for a cause that is greater than themselves.[28] The servant leader sees the community as a means to influence the larger population in order to promote a better society. They dedicate themselves to putting into practice all of the previous nine characteristics in order to change the larger community for the better. For Christian servant leaders, they are concerned with living a Christ-centered life together with other believers. This is more commonly known as the church.

> Let us hold unswervingly to the hope we profess, for He who promised is faithful. And let us consider how we may spur one another on toward love and good deeds, not giving up meeting together, as some are in the habit of doing. But encouraging one another—and all the more as you see the Day approaching. (Hebrews 10:23–25)

What an absolutely beautiful picture of community—believers standing together for a common purpose that is much larger than anything they could do on their own. Servant leaders see the need for this kind of community and pull people together because they see the value in it.

Final Thoughts on Servant Leadership

As this chapter has shown, servant leadership is threaded throughout the Bible. It is not surprising that Robert

Greenleaf recognized the value of self-sacrificing, service-oriented leadership through the organizational values of the Christian church. So much of the Bible demonstrates the necessity of having a servant's heart and following with a servant's heart that it makes sense to lead this way as well.

The binding agent of servant leadership is really the revolving pursuit to put followers at the center. When the leader decides that followers' interests are greater than their own, they have taken a step toward the ultimate fulfilment of servant leadership.[29] It is no wonder why one may see this type of leadership in Jesus. Although His followers did not readily recognize it, they had a need that was greater than His own. They (we) needed an unhindered road toward God, and He sacrificed Himself to make it possible. God stepped in to ensure His followers could be successful. He demonstrated the servant leadership not only by what He taught but also by what He did in His actions. This is, like so many other leadership styles, is the essence of what it means not only to be a Christ-follower but a leader for Christ.

> Greater love has no one than this: to lay down one's life for one's friends. (John 15:13)

Chapter Notes

[1] P. Northouse, *Leadership Theory and Practice,* seventh edition (Los Angeles, CA: Sage, 2016), 225.

[2]   D. Frick, *Robert K. Greenleaf: A Life of Servant Leadership* (San Francisco, CA: Berrett-Koehler Publishers, 2004), 45.

[3]   D. Frick, *Robert K. Greenleaf,* 17.

[4]   D. Frick, *Robert K. Greenleaf,* 17.

[5]   D. Frick, *Robert K. Greenleaf,* 125–31.

[6]   Y. Chung, "Why Servant Leadership? Its Uniqueness and Principles in the Life of Jesus," *Journal of Asia Adventist Seminary, 14*(2): 159–70 (2011).

[7]   K. Blanchard and P. Hodges, *The Servant Leader: Transforming Your Heart, Hands, Head, and Habits* (Nashville, TN: Countryman, 2003), 20–21.

[8]   L. Spears, "Practicing Servant Leadership," *Leader to Leader, 34*: 7–11, (2004). In this work, Spears reiterates his findings of servant leadership characteristics. Also in P. Northouse, *Leadership Theory and Practice,* 227. Northouse credits Spears with identifying these ten characteristics for practitioner purposes.

[9]   L. Spears, "Practicing Servant Leadership," 8.

[10] P. Northouse, *Leadership Theory and Practice,* 227.

[11] L. Spears, "Practicing Servant Leadership," p. 8 and P. Northouse, *Leadership,* 227.

[12] L. Spears, "Practicing Servant Leadership," 9.

[13] N. Burton, "Empathy vs. Sympathy," *Psychology Today* (May 2015), retrieved from https://www.psychologytoday.com/blog/hide-and-seek/201505/empathy-vs-sympathy. In this article, Burton delineates between the progressive order of emotions toward those suffering. The progression begins with pity, then leads to sympathy, empathy, and compassion.

[14] L. Spears, "Practicing Servant Leadership," 9.

[15] P. Northouse, *Leadership,* 228.

[16] L. Spears, "Practicing Servant Leadership," 9.

[17] D. Frick, *Robert K. Greenleaf,* 129–30.

[18] See Acts 17:16–34.

[19] P. Northouse, *Leadership,* 228.

[20] M. Hackman and C. Johnson, *Leadership: A Communication Perspective*, sixth edition (Long Grove, IL: Waveland Press, 2013), 112.

[21] J. Kouzes and B. Posner, *The Leadership Challenge*, fifth edition (San Francisco, CA: The Leadership Challenge, 2010), 131.

[22] See Matthew 4:19; Mark 1:17.

[23] P. Northouse, *Leadership*, 228.

[24] T. Sanders, *Strategic Thinking and the New Science: Planning in the Midst of Chaos, Complexity, and Change* (New York, Free Press, 1998), 110.

[25] L. Spears, "Practicing Servant Leadership," 9.

[26] P. Northouse, *Leadership*, 229.

[27] See Acts 18:24–28.

[28] P. Northouse, *Leadership*, 229.

[29] P. Northouse, *Leadership*, 234.

7

Conclusion

As has been demonstrated, there are scores of leadership styles, traits, theories, and types. The surface has scarcely been touched, and as many have pointed out, leadership is a commodity almost certainly left to interpretation at times. What this book has attempted to do is bring leadership under the realm of God and His word in order to understand how so many different academic definitions and illustrations may be found in Scripture. Just as the world vies for leaders, so does the church. To be made in the image of God is to be made in the image of a leader. Each church member must understand what his or her role is in leadership and apply in a manner that 1) brings glory to God and 2) supports and encourages the body.

The remainder of this work will highlight some important topics that must be considered with regard to leadership. To be sure, they are important because they underpin some often-forgotten or overlooked aspects of leadership. In this concluding chapter, gender, ethics, and the Holy Spirit will be discussed to see how these impact individual and corporate leadership. These are not all-encompassing topics, but they should offer a perspective on their relevance and importance when it comes to leadership and the Bible. It may be helpful to revisit or think back on the previous chapters to get the most out of this one.

Gender Considerations

There will be a day when everything is made perfect and whole and clear. Until then, leaders have an obligation to ensure certain issues do not remain silent. Gender has been the topic of discussion for many years, and it warrants its own section, if not chapter. The purpose of this section is to demonstrate how gender roles, especially in leadership, complement one another. Some believe that the church and the Bible is a man's domain, but this is not the total truth. The Bible has much to say on women in leadership.

To be completely honest would be to admit that women are not considered for some leadership positions because of stereotypical prejudice and unwarranted bias.[1] It must also be noted that I believe there is precedence set in the Bible when it comes to men and women in the church, but it does not preclude women from taking leadership roles.[2] Studies have indicated that there are certain traits, such as nurturing, that may be higher in women than in men, and there may be traits in men that are higher than in women. In any case, the differences between men and women are important because leaders' behavioral styles are detrimental to success as a leader.[3]

This section will not discuss the differences between women and men, however. It will discuss the importance of both.

To begin with, the book of Judges offers an excellent example of women in leadership. God raised up a woman judge over Israel who would give godly leadership to a man in order to defeat Israel's enemies. Under Deborah's leadership, God granted Israel forty years of peace and rest. She judged according to God's leadership and, in turn, provided godly leadership to Barak. Upon their victory over the Canaanite king, they sang a song known as the "Song of Deborah." The song begins, "When leaders lead in Israel ..."[4] What a testament to women leaders. This demonstrates that God raises up whomever He chooses to raise up for His purposes.

There is much Scripture pointing to Christian equality—living under the same Lord and receiving His gifts and blessings accordingly—and this must be kept in mind when teaching new leaders. Leadership has no boundaries when it comes to gender. Boundaries are set by the leaders themselves, male or female. Each leader has a responsibility to bring up the next leader. This is the limit of gender leadership. In fact, when it comes to leadership and gender, it simply means leadership. No one denies that women and men sometimes lead differently, but some men lead differently than other men. The key is to remain faithful to God as a leader.

In writing his final letter to his protégé Timothy, Paul does not mention the godly leadership Timothy's father taught him:

> I am reminded of your sincere faith,
> which first lived in your grandmother
> Lois and in your mother Eunice and, I
> am persuaded, now lives in you also. (2
> Timothy 1:5)

Paul's testimony is to the women that led Timothy to have such great faith. Paul recognized that leadership is not partial to gender, and it is best initiated by respecting gender roles. For example, in 1 Thessalonians 2:7 and 11 Paul writes that he and the other apostles led the Thessalonians with the character of a mother and father. In this Paul explains that it took the leadership qualities of both a woman and a man to minister to them properly.

Ethics

One definition of ethics is a standard of moral conduct and judgments about whether human behavior is right or wrong.[5] This definition broad strokes ethics as an ideal leaders must not only consider, but they must also adhere to. The ethical leader takes into account others' morality as well as their own. Since leadership is never about having a "do as I say, not as I do" attitude, those who practice this must evaluate the ethical dilemma they are conveying to their followers. This type of attitude is contrary to most leadership styles and does not show respect for followers' sense of right and wrong.

Most scholars would say that ethics is demonstrated through leaders' ability to treat followers with dignity and respect, as well as recognizing each person's uniqueness as an individual.[6] There is merit in this thought, but it must be mentioned that the Christian leader must never serve a person's uniqueness over God's design for people. Nevertheless, no matter a person's uniqueness, the Bible clearly teaches that we must show dignity and respect to one another as human beings serving a loving and just God. For example, imagine what might have happened if Jesus had not shown dignity and respect to the Samaritan woman at the well. Jesus, considered a Jewish teacher, had no problem speaking with a lone and seemingly promiscuous Samaritan woman to lead her to a saving knowledge of the Christ.[7] He certainly had respect for her as a human being and showed her dignity by not turning away from her. Jesus also recognized her uniqueness and responded appropriately. This is the kind of ethical behavior God calls each person to. This is the kind of ethical behavior that compassion stems from.

Effervescing: Leading from the Spirit

One might think of a round tablet that bubbles vigorously when dropped in a glass of water; emitting gases that work powerfully to aid in the relief of internal discomfort. The same idea is meant here. When the Holy Spirit regenerates and indwells us, we should be compelled to exude Him from our very being. The relief He brings to each of us who have Him is the same relief He brings to others when we follow His leading. People need to see the Holy Spirit effervescing from our leadership as much as we need the Holy Spirit to effervesce through our leadership.

In each leadership style, there has been a common thread running through each: the relationship between the leader and follower. In each case, the leader has to make a concerted effort to do right by God, their followers, and themselves. The only way to accomplish this with continued success is to rely upon the Holy Spirit to guide actions and decisions as they are made. As leaders, the Holy Spirit is our guided to be great leaders.

> For we know, brothers loved by God, that He has chosen you, because our gospel came to you not simply with words, but also with power, with the Holy Spirit and with deep conviction. You know how we lived among you for your sake. You became imitators of us and of the Lord: in spite of our suffering, you welcomed the message with the joy given by the Holy Spirit. (1 Thessalonians 1:4–6)

When the previous passage is examined, there is a powerful message about leading according to the Holy Spirit. Paul credits the Holy Spirit in these few verses by enabling him and Silas and Timothy with leadership abilities, passion to preach, endurance through circumstance, exemplary example, and joy unto others. It is because of these attributes that others desired to follow their example—it is because of the Holy Spirit.

On a broader level, spirituality in general is being credited for helping to develop leaders in ways that keep them attuned to morality, developing virtues that impact others positively, becoming more benevolent in action, and helping to develop an overall organizational climate that impacts cohesiveness, trustworthiness, and humility.[8] For the Christian leader, this means deriving spirituality from the Holy Spirit's leading. Each person is set on a journey of spiritual formation. The deeper and more attentive to this journey leaders are, the more they effervesce the Spirit.

What's Next?

The hope is that this book has given leaders insight into what best fits them in the circumstances they are in. This has not been an argument to discover which style or theory is better than the other. It is meant to allow leaders to discover where their strengths and weaknesses settle. It is meant to give Christian leaders the understanding of what they can do to enhance their own leadership. There is one final segment to help in this endeavor.

For every leader to be effective, it is not enough to simply know what the styles and theories are, but they must know how they possess them and how to improve upon them. First, there is the matter of prayer unto wisdom. Remember that James tells us that those who seek godly wisdom for His purposes alone will receive it abundantly.[9] Each of us must make the effort to know God's will for our particular leadership.

Next, there is the need to continually develop our leadership, not only through other leaders but from followers as well. The idea is leadership tells us that when feedback is sought from those within our sphere of influence and connection, we become more astute and aware of what others think of our leadership. Leaders need to know how they are leading according to others to work on areas that need improvement.

Finally, leaders need to take a good look at themselves and determine what the goals are for organizations, for others, and for themselves. Once they have a good grasp on this, then they can move toward improving their leadership. One way to help take a good look at personal leadership style is to take self and follower evaluation surveys. These surveys are developed to identify areas for sustainment, areas for improvement, strengths, and weaknesses. Leadership assessments are a great way to understand personal emphasis.

The leader's work is never done, especially as a Christian leader. Leadership has a responsibility to endure for the sake of followership. Again, it does not matter if one is leading change as a transformational leader, if one leads *quid pro quo* as a transactional leader, or if one centers around the follower as a servant leader, each must do right according to God—because every Christian has potential to be a leader for God.

> And whatever you do, whether in word
> or deed, do it all in the name of the Lord
> Jesus, giving thanks to God the Father
> through Him. (Colossians 3:17)

Chapter Notes

---

1   P. Northouse, *Leadership Theory and Practice*, seventh edition (Los Angeles, CA: Sage, 2016), 404.

2   I believe the Bible speaks to God giving leadership responsibility to men over women when it comes to obedience in partnership, relationships, and the church. For example, Genesis 3 illustrates Eve's sin in the garden, but also Adam's responsibility as the family leader. Neither escaped consequence, but Adam was ultimately at fault. I believe this demonstrates a picture of family and church. Although both men and women answer to God, and are accountable for their individual actions, when paired, God will hold men more responsible over women.

3   I. Cuadrado, C. Garcia-Ael, and F. Molero, "Gender Typing of Leadership: Evaluations of Real and Ideal Managers," *Scandinavian Journal of Psychology*, 56 (2015): 236–44.

4   See Judges 4:1—5:31.

5   M. Hackman and C. Johnson, *Leadership: A Communication Perspective*, sixth edition (Long Grove, IL: Waveland, 2013), 336.

6   P. Northouse, *Leadership Theory and Practice*, 336.

7   See John 4.

8   M. Hackman and C. Johnson, *Leadership: A Communication Perspective*, 395.

9   James 1:5

Bibliography

Arkush, A. "Voltaire on Judaism and Christianity." *ASJ Review, 18*, no. 2 (1993): 223–43. Accessed March 18, 2017. From http://0-eds.a.ebscohost.com.library. regent. edu/ehost/detail/detail? vid=3&sid=8fc82d20-0616-489d-afa8-24030d09c51f% 40sessionmgr4008 &hid=4203&b data =JnN pdGU9ZW hvc3QtbGl2 ZQ%3d%3d#AN= ATLA0001767832&db=rfh.

Avolio, B. and B. Bass. *Developing Potential Across a Full Range of Leadership™: Cases on Transactional and Transformational Leadership.* Mahwah, NJ: LEA Publishers, 2002.

Bass, B. and R. Riggio. *Transformational Leadership,* second edition. Mahwah, New Jersey: LEA Publishers, 2006.

Bass, B. and R. Stogdill. *Bass & Stogdill's Handbook of Leadership: Theory, Research, and Managerial Applications.* New York: The Free Press, 1990.

Blake, R. and J. Mouton. "An overview of the Grid®." *Training and Development Journal, 29,* No.5 (1975): 29–38. Accessed March 18, 2017. From http://0-eds.a.ebscohost.com.library.regent.edu /ehost/ detail/ detail?vid=11&sid=19e8b36d-e47d-4b44-99a5-1a27

96cd50b0% 40sessionmgr4006&hid=4203& bdata=
JnNpdGU9 ZWhvc3QtbGl2ZQ% 3d%3d#db=a9h
&AN=7447702.

Blanchard, K. *Leading at a Higher Level*, Revised. Upper Saddle River, NJ: FT Press, 2010.

Blanchard, K. and P. Hodges. *The Servant Leader: Transforming Your Heart, Hands, Head, and Habits.* Nashville, TN: Countryman, 2003.

Burke, W. *Organization Change: Theory and Practice*, fourth edition. Los Angeles, CA: Sage, 2014.

Burns, J. *Leadership.* New York: Harper & Row, 1978.

Burton, N. "Empathy vs. Sympathy," *Psychology Today.* (May 2015). Accessed on March 18, 2017. From https://www. psychologytoday.com /blog/hide-and-seek/201505/ empathy-vs-sympathy.

Chan, A., S. Hannah, and W. Gardner. "Veritable Authentic Leadership: Emergence, Functioning, and Impacts." In *Authentic Leadership Theory and Practice: Origin, Effects, and Development*, ed. B. Avolio, W. Gardner, and F. Walumbwa. From *Monographs in Leadership and Management*, vol. 3, edited by J. Hunt. San Diego, CA: Elsevier, 2005.

Chung, Y. "Why Servant Leadership? Its Uniqueness and Principles in the Life of Jesus." *Journal of Asia Adventist Seminary, 14*, No. 2 (2011): 159–70. Accessed March 18, 2017. From http://0-eds.a.ebscohost. com. library. regent.edu/ehost/detail/detail? vid=14& sid=19e8b36d-e47d-4b44-99a5-1a2796cd50b0% 40sessionmgr4006 &hid=4203&bdata=JnNpd GU9 ZW hvc3QtbGl2ZQ %3d%3d#AN=88804903& db=a9h.

Collins, K. *John Wesley: A Theological Journey.* Nashville, TN: Abingdon Press, 2003.

Cuadrado, I., C. Garcia-Ael, and F. Molero. "Gender Typing of Leadership: Evaluations of Real and Ideal Managers." *Scandinavian Journal of Psychology,* 56. (2015): 236–44. Accessed March 18, 2017. From http://0-eds.a. ebscohost.com.Library.regent. edu/ehost/detail/detail?   vid=16&sid=19e8b36d-e47d-4 b44-99a5-1a2796cd 50 b0%40 sessionmgr 4006&hid=4203&bdata = JnNpd GU9Z Whvc3Qtb Gl2ZQ%3d%3d#AN=101470395&db=a9h.

Darnton, R. "Voltaire, Historian." *Raritan, 35,* No. 2 (2015): 20–28. Rutgers University. Accessed March 18, 2017. From Regent University.

Elmer, D. *Cross-Cultural Communication.* Downers Grove, IL: IVP Academic, 2002.

Englebrecht, E. ed. *The Church from Age to Age: A History from Galilee to Global Christianity.* Saint Louis, MO: Concordia Publishing House, 2011.

Frick, D. *Robert K. Greenleaf: A Life of Servant Leadership.* San Francisco: Berrett-Koehler Publishers, 2004.

Gaebelein, F. ed. *The Expositor's Bible Commentary.* Volume 8. Grand Rapids, MI: Zondervan, 1984.

George, B. *Authentic Leadership: Rediscovering the Secrets to Building Lasting Value.* San Francisco: Jossey-Bass, 2003. Referenced in P. Northouse. *Leadership Theory and Practice,* seventh edition. Los Angeles, CA: Sage, 2016.

George, B. and P. Sims. *True North: Discover Your Authentic Leadership.* San Francisco, CA: Jossey-Bass, 2007.

Global Leadership Summit. Accessed on March 18, 2017. From www.willowcreek.com/events/leadership.

Hackman, M. and C. Johnson. *Leadership: A Communication Perspective*, sixth edition. Long Grove, IL: Waveland, 2013.

Hamstra, M., N. Yperen, B. Wisse, and K. Sassenberg. "Transformational and transactional leadership and followers' achievement goals." *Journal of Business Psychology, 29* (2014): 413–25. Accessed March 18, 2017. From http://0-eds.a.ebscohost.com.library.regent. edu/ehost/detail/ detail?vid=26&sid =19e8b36d-e47d-4b44-99a5-1a2796cd50b0%40 sessionmgr 4006&hid= 4203&bdata=JnNpdGU9ZWhvc3Q tbGl2ZQ%3d%3d#AN=97411916&db=a9h.

History Staff. "Enlightenment." (2009). Accessed March 18, 2017. From History.com.

House, R. "Path-goal theory of leadership: lessons, legacy, and reformulated theory." *Leadership Quarterly, 7.* No. 3 (1996): 326. Accessed March 18, 2017. From Regent University.

Ike, O. "Core Values for Responsible Leadership: The Relevance of Ethics for Religion and Development." *The Ecumenical Review, 68*, No. 4 (2017): 463–71. Accessed March 18, 2017. From http://0-eds.a.ebscohost. com.library.regent.edu/ ehost/detail/detail ?vid=31&sid= 19e8b36d-e47d-4b44-99a5-1a2796cd50b0 %40 sessionmgr4006& hid=4203&bdata= JnNpdGU9ZWhvc 3Qt bGl2ZQ%3d%3d#AN=120629231&db=a9h.

Katz, R. "Skills of an effective administrator." *Harvard Business Review, 52*, No. 5 (1974): 91. Accessed March 18, 2017. From Regent University.

Kouzes, J. and B. Posner. *The Leadership Challenge*, fifth edition. San Francisco: Wiley, 2012.

Kreitner, R. and A. Kinicki. *Organizational Behavior*, tenth edition. New York: McGraw-Hill Irvine, 2013.

Lloyd-Jones, M. *Luther and His Message for Today*. Evangelical Press, 1968. In M. Noll, *Turning Points: Decisive Moments in the History of Christianity*, second edition. Grand Rapids, MI: Baker Academic, 2000.

Luther, M. "A Sermon on Keeping Children in School." In M. Noll, *Turning Points: Decisive Moments in the History of Christianity*, second edition. Grand Rapids, MI: Baker Academic, 2000.

Matheson, P. ed. *Reformation Christianity.* In A People's History of Christianity, vol. 5. Minneapolis, MN: Augsburg Fortress Press, 2010.

Mumford, M., S. Zaccaro, M. Connelly, and M. Marks. "Leadership skills: conclusions and future directions." *Leadership Quarterly, 11*, No.1 (2000): 155–70. Accessed March 18, 2017. From Regent University.

Mumford, M., S. Zaccaro, F. Harding, T. Jacobs, and E. Fleishman. "Leadership skills for a changing world: Solving complex social problems." *Leadership Quarterly, 11*, No. 1 (2000): 11–35. Accessed March 18, 2017. From Regent University.

Noll, M. *Turning Points: Decisive Moments in the History of Christianity*, second edition. Grand Rapids, MI: Baker Academic, 2000.

Northouse, P. *Leadership: Theory and Practice*, seventh edition. Los Angeles, CA: Sage, 2015.

Oster, G. *The Light Prize: Perspectives on Christian Innovation.* Virginia Beach, VA: Positive Signs Media, 2011.

Rodrigues, A. and M. Ferreira. "The impact of transactional and transformational leadership style on organizational citizenship behavior." *Psico-USF,* *20,* No. 3(2015): 493–504. Accessed March 18, 2017. From http://0-eds.a.ebscohost.com.library. regent. edu/ehost/detail/detail? vid=36&sid=19e8b36d-e47d-4b44-99a5-1a2796cd50b0 %40 sessionmgr 4006&hid=4203&bdata= JnNpdGU9 ZWhvc3Qtb Gl2ZQ%3d%3d#AN=112076596&db=a9h.

Sanders, J. O. *Spiritual Leadership: Principles of Excellence for Every Believer.* Chicago: Moody Publishers, 2007.

Sanders, T. *Strategic Thinking and the New Science: Planning in the Midst of Chaos, Complexity, and Chang.* New York, Free Press, 1998.

Sears, G. and R. Hackett. "The Influence of Role Definition and Affect in LMX: A Process Perspective on the Personality-LMX Relationship." *Journal of Occupational and Organizational Psychology,* *84* (2011): 544–64. Accessed March 18, 2017. From http://0-eds.a.ebscohost. com.library.regent. edu/ehost/detail/ detail?vid=40&sid= 19e8b36d-e47d-4b44-99a5-1a2796 cd50b 0%40sessionmg r4006&hid=4203&bdata=Jn NpdGU9ZW hvc3Qtb Gl2ZQ%3d%3d#AN=70118464&db=a9h.

Shelley, B. *Church History in Plain Language,* third edition. Nashville, TN: Thomas Nelson, 2008.

Spears, L. "Practicing Servant Leadership." *Leader to Leader,* *34* (2004): 7–11. Accessed March 18, 2017. From http://0-eds.a. ebscohost.com. library.

regent.edu/e host/detail/detail?vid=42&sid= 19e8b 36d-e47d-4b44-99a5-1a2796cd50b0%40sessionmgr 4006&hid=4203 &bdata=JnNpd GU9ZWhvc3Q tbGl2ZQ %3d%3d#AN= 17070251&db=a9h.

Stock, R. M. and G. Ozbek-Pothoff. "Implicit leadership in an intercultural context: theory extension and empirical investigation." *International Journal of Human Resource Management*, 25, No. 2 (2014): 1651–68. Accessed March 18, 2017. From Regent University.

Tzinerr, A. and L. Barsheshet-Picker. "Authentic Management as a Moderator of the Relationship between the Congruence of Gender Role Identity-Gender Management Characteristics, and Leader-Member Exchange (LMX)." *Journal of Work and Organizational Psychology*, 30 (2014): 49–60. Accessed March 18, 2017. From http://0-eds.a.ebsco host.com.library.regent.edu/ehost/ detail/detail? vid= 45&sid=19e8b36d-e47d-4b44-99a5-1a2796cd50b0% 40sessionmgr4006&hid=4203&bdata=JnNpdGU9 ZWhvc3QtbGl2ZQ%3d%3d#AN=97293669& db=a9h.

Valantasis, R. "Body, hierarchy, and leadership in Chrysostom's 'On the Priesthood." *Greek Orthodox Theological Review*, 30 No. 4 (1985): 455–71. Accessed March 18, 2017. From Regent University.

Vandegrift, R. and J. Matusitz. "Path-goal theory: a successful Columbia Records story." *Journal of Human Behavior in the Social Environment*, 21 (2011): 350–62. Accessed March 18, 2017. From http://0-eds.a.ebscohost.com.   library.regent.edu/ehost/

detail/ detail?vid=3&sid=9a5300 ce-b09c-49d7-acaa-
ea5831aa439d% 40sessionmgr 4007&hid=420 &
bdata=JnNpdGU9ZWhvc3QtbGl2Z Q%3d%3d#
AN=60828144&db=a9h.

Walumbwa, F., B. Avolio, W. Gardner, T. Wernsing, and
S. Peterson. "Authentic Leadership: Development
and Validation of a Theory-Based Measure." *Journal
of Management*, *34* No. 1 (2008): 89–126. Accessed
March 18, 2017. From Regent University.

About the Author

Ryan retired from the United States Marine Corps in 2014 after serving more than 18 years'. He was privileged to lead, follow, and serve in garrison and combat with extraordinary individuals. Ryan completed a Bachelors in Christian Studies and a Masters in Organizational Leadership. Currently, Ryan is a pastor on the Southern Oregon coast where he, his wife of 19 years', and three children live.

Printed in the United States
By Bookmasters